America's Culture of Professionalism

America's Culture of Professionalism

Past, Present, and Prospects

David Warfield Brown

palgrave
macmillan

First published in 2014 by PALGRAVE MACMILLAN® in the United States—a division of St. Martin's Press LLC, 175 Fifth Avenue, New York, NY 10010.

Where this book is distributed in the UK, Europe and the rest of the world, this is by Palgrave Macmillan, a division of Macmillan Publishers Limited, registered in England, company number 785998, of Houndmills, Basingstoke, Hampshire RG21 6XS.

Palgrave Macmillan is the global academic imprint of the above companies and has companies and representatives throughout the world.

Palgrave® and Macmillan® are registered trademarks in the United States, the United Kingdom, Europe and other countries.

ISBN: 978-1-137-34191-4

Library of Congress Cataloging-in-Publication Data

Brown, David Warfield.
    America's culture of professionalism : past, present, and prospects / David Warfield Brown.
        pages cm
    Includes bibliographical references and index.
        ISBN 978-1-137-34191-4 (hardback : alk. paper) 1. Professional employees—United States. I. Title.
    HD8038.U5B76 2014
    306.3′613—dc23

                                                                2013050464

A catalogue record of the book is available from the British Library.

Design by Amnet.

First edition: June 2014

10 9 8 7 6 5 4 3 2 1

Contents

Preface

I remember William Faulkner telling me, "When the bug bites, you'll write." That was at a time when I favored the life of a writer; but after several polite rejections from *The New Yorker*, I decided that to feed myself perhaps the law was a better meal. So I entered willingly into America's culture of professionalism, via the legal profession; well fed but, as I came to learn, undernourished. Such a culture does not encourage the "personal" and for me that left too much out and leaves too many others out. Now the bug has bitten again and the itch I've had for the past thirty years about our culture is the centerpiece of this book.

Professionalism itself is neither good nor bad; how it's practiced is what really matters. For too long I had been immodest enough to think I had little to learn from those who were not my professional "peers." I entertained an unexamined pretension that I knew far more than I actually did. It was a mind-set that became a kind of confinement limiting my intellectual and moral development. I remember sitting on our Hamptons sundeck and thinking to myself that for too long "acting professionally" had left me in shallow waters. Eventually I stepped away from top-down government positions and the practice of law to find the time and place for serious reconsideration of America's culture of professionalism. I had too easily taken for granted that credentials were a sufficient trump card; but the truth is that those in the "Emerald City" are not wizards at all:

"Making believe," cried Dorothy. "Are you not a great Wizard?"

"Hush, my dear," he said; "don't speak so loud. Or you will be overheard—and I should be ruined. I'm supposed to be a great Wizard."

"And aren't you?" she asked.

"Not a bit of it, my dear; I'm just a common man." (L. Frank Baum, *The Wizard of Oz*)

And so I began to turn my attention to writing again and also to teaching, so I could share what I had learned and to explore what I had yet to learn. My intellectual and moral development found academe a valuable intersection for both. I chose to make myself vulnerable again—teaching will do that if you are really serious about learning. When I boarded the mother ship of professionalism—the American graduate school—I found that problem solving more often than not was knowledge-based rather than people-based. My research became centered on the social dimensions of problem solving. I told my students that the specialized methods they acquired in graduate school were likely to appear as closed systems with no admittance to those who were not professionals. I told them that although professionals routinely share and "solve" problems together in their respective niches, they also share an economic incentive to exclude those without credentials. Although as a recovering professional I was still a work in progress, I recalled my correspondence with Parker Palmer and told my students they should know that the answers are not "out there," where power and expertise reside, or "in here," where each individual resides, but "between us." I wanted them to consider knowledge construction as a social process instead of a credentialed possession. My teaching also gave me the opportunity to create and experiment with cases and group exercises to help students better understand the social dynamics of real-world problem solving after too many years of schooling where they were expected to succeed on their own. I saw that their journeys, like mine, might very well take them to a place where everyone counts; a place that too many "professionals" in government, the large nonprofits, and higher education have yet to discover.

Through teaching, I learned a great deal more about academe from colleagues and students that helped to shape the arguments in this volume. I also learned that academe had become increasingly preoccupied with preparing students to make a living, and not how to live. I thought there should be room for a discussion about human ends as well as human means. In my mind, without that conversation there was really only training, not education. Self-interest may be a starting point for faculty and students but not necessarily the fixed or exclusive destination. With more time to write, which also meant more time to think, I found myself fashioning short pieces that eventually led to this volume. My moral development also came more easily as I discovered that "acting professionally" did not necessarily qualify as virtuous behavior. My goal is to clarify what

I learned on my journey as a recovering professional and to consider the following:

1. Why do so many in academe treat knowledge as a form of property? This question leads me to explore knowledge as a social construct emerging from a variety of collaborative sources *beyond* academe.
2. Why do so many credentialed "experts" assume that they have sufficient knowledge to address public problems, ignoring the potential of citizen collaboration? This leads me to the concept of a no-man's land, largely unoccupied except for the precedent of America's jury system, where professionals and citizens as jurors deliberate together as equals.
3. What can be done when so many professionals have allowed their self-interest to exploit those they serve? This leads me to explore new forms of collaboration emerging between those I think of as "new professionals" and laypersons with such "new professionals" nurturing the capacities of those they serve rather than prolonging their dependence; working *with* them, not just *for* them, and learning *from* them, not just offering advice.

My research and examination here cover both the academic world—the "home office" of professionalism—and the social dimensions of problem solving in the public world beyond academe. It is where these two worlds meet, or fail to meet, that shapes the book's argument. I think the culture of professionalism should be seriously examined and reconsidered by researchers, professors, students, and members of the general public. All of whom are responsible for what it has become and, more important, what it yet may be.

Acknowledgments

Acknowledgments often end with some warm words for a spouse who put up with the author's undertaking. Here, I want to begin with my respect and gratitude for my wife Alice, whose "professional" attention to my manuscript has been critically important. As an English teacher for many years, Alice used her practiced and careful eye for what could make a better sentence, paragraph, or chapter. I am always learning from Alice in so many ways.

Over the years, I also learned so much from so many that, again, my respect and gratitude run deep and lasting. For this particular work, I remember with special thanks what I learned from David Riesman, Larry Cremin, Charles Lindblom, Parker Palmer, and David Mathews—all, in their own special ways, critics of America's culture of professionalism. And, of course, I should acknowledge what I learned over the years from my colleagues in law practice, government service, academe, and those associated with the Kettering Foundation—all of whom shared in my intellectual journey as a "recovering professional."

Putting this manuscript together I profited from the generous interest of Valentina Tursini, a former editor of mine, who went out of her way to help me clarify many things. And there was Charlotte Maiorana and Leila Campoli who initially brought me into the Palgrave house, and my editors, Brian Foster and Casie Vogel, and editorial assistants, Sarah Lawrence, Rachel Taenzler, and Bradley Showalter, who helped bring the manuscript the rest of the way. I also want to thank those in academe and elsewhere who contributed their thoughts as I put together my work here: Anna Brown, Isaiah Brown, Martin Carcasson, Jeremy Cohen, David Cooper, Joni Doherty, Albert Dzur, Julie Ellison, Don Flory, Tom Hassan, Elizabeth Minnich, Mary Ann Murphy, KerryAnn O'Meara, Bernie Ronan, Richard Schubart, Wick Sloane, and Randy Watt.

America's culture of professionalism cannot be easily captured between the covers of a book any more than my thanks to so many can be captured in my acknowledgments here. But let me conclude by giving thanks for our son Peter and daughter Sarah, who have always gone out of their way to extend their love when it has been most needed. I have learned from them, too, what no book will ever capture.

Introduction

For more than a century in an increasingly complex society, the culture of professionalism has steadily seized the high ground in higher education, government, and the marketplace with its multitude of self-anointed "professional" occupations. It is a culture that transcends both political left and right, as most Americans have no settled rank by birth or class and have to make a "place" for themselves. Is it any wonder then that the United States is supposedly the most professionalized country in the world?

The culture of professionalism has become so dominant in American life that, ironically, it has become invisible to most people. That is why one rarely finds "professional" or "professionalism" in any book index—a reflection of how little thought is given to what such terms mean and their almost undisputed and reigning presence in so many lives. Professionalism has become something of an ideology, beyond the realm of rethinking; and "acting professionally" or being a "consummate professional" has become an unquestioned standard of conduct. Those who think of themselves as "professionals"—both scholars and those in professional practice—presume that they share specialized knowledge with like-minded colleagues, which serves the interests of students, clients, patients, and other publics. Since most nonprofessionals presume they cannot manage without such help, the culture of professionalism goes relatively unquestioned. To borrow from Eva Brann, I think professionalism "is no longer in a state of inquiry," but it should be.[1]

Culture is a difficult concept to understand. Consider the example of social conventions as a way of bringing culture into more everyday view. Social conventions are daily habits of coordination, such as forming a line, that have become "accepted and established solutions to past recurrent coordination problems which—with time—assume the status of norms."[2] Like norms, a culture does not arise at one specific time and is the result of "complex patterns of behavior of a large number of people over a protracted period of time."[3] A culture then, like social conventions, is learned behavior—it is what we learn from the examples of others—it is not the product of reason. It is not chosen. It evolves.[4] But once established, a culture finds raw expression when someone says, "that's just the way we do things around here."

Academe has nurtured a culture that is so deeply embedded that most academics and professionals rarely entertain critical moments of analysis and reconsideration of it. Why is that? At the heart of the culture of professionalism are widely held assumptions about what is important, promoting a conformity among those who seek acceptance. Such assumptions are not explicitly acknowledged and yet powerfully shape how scholars and practicing professionals operate. They include sharing a "common language and concepts," establishing "group boundaries" that include some and exclude others, and determining "how rewards and status are allocated."[5] In addition, such assumptions are the hard evidence of what has stood the test of time, much like what I have called "metaconventions" or precepts of behavior that explain, for example, why we form lines ("first come, first served").

Where is the culture of professionalism learned? First, in schools and universities, where students learn from the example of their teachers and professors. To become a "professional" requires first obtaining certain pieces of knowledge, which most people don't have, and making a living on their belief that what a professional knows is important for their well-being. For those who do not become "professionals," there are a hundred different shaping sources beyond their schooling to reinforce what they learned about how to behave in a culture of professionalism—to assume that pieces of knowledge are forms of property that belong to somebody else, and to delegate problems to those who they think have answers.

Professionalism is thoroughly in accord with those who have respect for merit, not class—status earned with, presumably, equality at the start for those seeking an education and the credentials it confers. Louis Menand points out that although "professions are democratic in the sense they are open to anyone with talent . . . they are [also] guilds in the sense that they protect their members from market forces with which all non-professionals have to cope."[6] Nonetheless, professionalism reinforces what most Americans have always valued: "the idea of work as a calling, a rationalist frame of mind, collective self-governance, and high levels of self direction in day-to-day work activities."[7] Jacques Barzun, however, saw professionalism as less than it professes to be: "It is to turn people who are not born teachers, born builders, born advocates, or born healers into a good imitation of the real thing. Easier said than done."[8]

Burton Clark offers the simple definition that a professional is someone whose "authority" is "rooted in expertise."[9] Thomas Haskell qualifies expertise: "Professionals are persons who claim to possess esoteric knowledge which serves as the basis for advice or services rendered to the public for remuneration."[10] And William Sullivan offered a more detailed definition of being a professional: "Professions are typically described as occupations characterized by three features: specialized training in a field of codified knowledge usually acquired by formal education and apprenticeship, public recognition of a certain autonomy on the part of the community of practitioners to regulate their own standards of practice, and commitment to provide service to the public beyond the economic welfare of practitioners."[11]

Putting aside such definitions, "professional" has become synonymous with "educated" and "competent." The title "professional" is liberally conferred with little reference to what someone actually does or how he does it, as long as they are good enough to get paid for it. Being considered a professional is a form of flattery as well as an expectation that quality service can be rendered. The claim of professionals knowing many things that others do not is, of course, superficially correct. However, being identified as a professional, and acquiring the status the title confers, depends, in part, on perpetuating some degree of mystery about what a particular "professional" actually does. Contributing to that mystery are academic or disciplinary assumptions that help to shape various forms of professional knowledge. Such assumptions are obviously of interest to academics but rarely examined by those who are professionals or those whose interests they ostensibly serve. As for undergraduate or graduate students who come under the sway of academics, such would-be professionals more or less take those assumptions for granted and continue to do so in practice.

And then there is the tacit knowledge acquired by professionals through experience, which is perhaps a more reliable asset than the esoteric knowledge that is normally associated with credentialed experts and is likely to be remote from those they serve. Harold Wilensky observed that most "professional knowledge, like all knowledge, is to some extent tacit and gives the established professions their aura of mystery."[12] However, what a professional has learned from experience is not necessarily beyond the understanding of those served but only separate and apart from their own experience. To say as Michael Polanyi does, that "there are things we know but cannot tell," does not make them necessarily mysterious but only more accessible to those who have actually experienced them.[13] Unfortunately, little is done to help those who have not pursued "professional" careers to make them more informed about the disciplinary assumptions and tacit knowledge of credentialed expertise, which would make the professional's expertise less mysterious.

Acquiring status is perhaps the most enduring mark of those claiming the professional mantle. Michael Walzer elaborates by saying: "Professional men and women have an interest in specifying the nature of their own performances, shucking off tasks that seem to them to be below the level of their training and certification."[14] To secure such status, "acting professionally" is a standard that most professionals observe and practice with great care. "Acting professionally" usually means keeping oneself out of whatever opinion or analysis is offered. Mary Ann Murphy, a professor of communication studies, noted that "the central component of professional behavior is the separation of personal feelings from decision making."[15] Her comment reminded me of an early critical piece I wrote on professionalism, which a colleague deemed "unprofessional." Why was it "unprofessional" in his mind? Well, I had told stories about myself, and for him that was much too personal. For many in academe, but not all, the assumption is that something personal is only "anecdotal," a pejorative term for anything that has not been replicated by an abundance of evidence that goes far beyond mere personal testimony. It is an assumption that is consistent with scientific rigor being the exemplary standard of those in academe. That's why Walker Percy once observed that science has nothing to say to the individual—"Science cannot utter a single word about an individual molecule, thing, or creature in so far as it is an individual but only in so far as it is like other individuals . . . [T]he layman is an individual. So science cannot say a single word to him or about him except as he resembles others."[16]

Acting "professionally" is not just a measure that professionals apply to themselves. It represents a standard of conduct that many others subscribe to. How often we hear, "Oh, she's a real professional," or "He did a very professional job." That may be one reason so many ambitious parents have become enamored with the goal of acquiring a professional identity and status for their children. These parents will do whatever is necessary to get their sons and daughters into the "best schools" so they are deemed worthy of a professional trajectory from kindergarten to graduate school with the reward of being considered a "professional" in whatever career they eventually choose to pursue.

PART I

The Culture of Professionalism

CHAPTER 1

Knowledge as Property

The Legacy of Self-Reliance

America's culture of professionalism has powerful ties to the country's legacy of self-reliance, which emerged in the early nineteenth century among new landowners and artisans. "Self-reliance" was famously celebrated in Ralph Waldo Emerson's 1841 essay, which was cobbled together from his lectures and journals of the 1830s. In his seclusion and self-absorption, Emerson was mainly addressing his own need to affirm himself, but the essay spoke to a fast-forming culture that was putting aside old world antecedents of "hireling" labor and replacing them with free bargaining agents. It was an ambitious culture of expansion that depended on men and women—both those of religious faith and those unsettled in their beliefs—who were determined to make a place for themselves without the promise of help extended by either church or state.[1]

Settling a new land and acquiring property was perhaps the most desirable way to facilitate and demonstrate self-reliance.[2] Property broadly understood was considered not so much a physical asset as it was a right to be exercised when such property was threatened by a competing interest or superior authority. In America's founding and expansion, property was a principal measure of one's standing and, yes, self-reliance. In his *Commentaries on the Laws of England* (1765–1769), William Blackstone put property at the center of human affairs: "There is nothing which so generally strikes the imagination, and engages the affections of mankind, as the right of property."[3] And Alexis de Tocqueville observed: "In no other country in the world is the love of property keener or more alert than in the United States."[4]

Self-reliance was undoubtedly necessary given the raw beginnings of land acquisition and emerging statehood. For at least some pioneers and settlers, the abundance of land and opportunities and the lack of a history to repudiate or reform made self-reliance more achievable. There was nothing to do but create whatever "Americans" wanted to pursue. Historian Robert Wiebe notes: "Everything depended on what individuals did for themselves. . . . Self-defined authority gave white men the mandate to rule collectively; self-directed work gave them the freedom to strike out individually. From one trunk came community self-governance, from the other economic self-determination."[5] There is abundant evidence, however, that self-reliance in this new land was enhanced by the cooperation of extended families and neighbors. Settlements became products of many hands working together, not just the property owner with his home as his "castle." It is a history that belies the oft-quoted "every man for himself." Sean Wilentz tells us that "contrary to still-persistent myths of rural rugged individualism, the yeoman households were tightly connected to each other—and increasingly to the outside world."[6]

Property and self-reliance, so dear in much of America's history, have always gone hand in hand. It may be why many professionals treat knowledge as a form of property. Both real property and specialized knowledge foster and reflect the desire and importance of self-reliance—especially in a young country like America where the cherished ideal of "liberty" has never been contested. Richard Flacks puts it this way: "Liberty idealizes self-sufficiency rather than interdependence . . . What is real and valuable for the authentic libertarian are the individual and his interests, not the society and its potential."[7] For Jedediah Purdy, property rights secure "not just exclusion of others from one's own space but command over the scope and character of activity there,"[8] which also describes the prerogatives of those who came to regard their specialized knowledge as a form of property.

The legacy of self-reliance certainly contributed to developing the culture of professionalism that emerged in the late nineteenth century. This culture was entirely consistent with the ideal of self-reliance in a young republic insofar as scholars and professional practitioners, by virtue of their specializations, were able to eventually secure positions that offered at least the appearance of being on one's own. Burton Bledstein vividly describes the self-reliance that a professional specialist acquired: He "resisted all corporate encroachments and regulations upon his independence, whether from government bureaucrats, university trustees, business administrators, public laymen, or even his own professional associations."[9] John Dewey offered an opaque description of a professional's false sense of self-sufficiency: "All specialization breeds a familiarity which tends to create an illusion. Material dealt with by specialized abstractive processes comes to have a psychological independence and completion which is converted—hypostatized—into objective independence and self-sufficiency."[10]

By the beginning of the twentieth century, the possession of knowledge as a form of property would rival the ownership of real property and its entitlements for those who would govern. Where real property was once the primary measure of a man's standing, proprietary knowledge and professional credentials became newly devised trump cards. Knowledge treated as a form of property in America's culture of professionalism became a means to secure the autonomy of scholars and the self-regulation of professional guilds. And the *status* of professionals was directly related to hard-won possessions that others came to respectfully acknowledge. "No Trespassing" signs were not necessary, as almost everyone accepted and observed such boundaries. The "progressive era" of the early twentieth century was the beginning of what would become the professional dominance of public life. However, treating knowledge as a form of property that "experts" acquired often resembled narrow strips of land, but when this view was applied to multidimensional problems it proved to be far from sufficient. Nonetheless, the time was not far off when many Americans would seek the advice and counsel of professionals for almost all of their daily concerns—how to raise their children, how to save their marriage, how to lose weight—an "outsourcing" that seems to have no end.[11]

Ironically, the culture of professionalism promoted layperson dependence—the antithesis of the long-held American ideal of self-reliance. To be self-reliant a professional found himself necessarily encouraging the dependence of others who had no such title or expertise. So treating knowledge as a form of property—held in common among professionals whether in the academy or within the practice of a profession—gave them the leverage to make a living by excluding those who lacked such knowledge. Consequently, the legacy of self-reliance was renewed and sustained among scholars and professional practitioners at the expense of a lay public that no longer thought it could navigate on its own.

Credentialed expertise as a new form of self-reliance was soon secured by self-regulating professional guilds as the like-minded drew together to organize. Through licensing, accreditation, and other forms of property-like monopoly, professionals made a secure place for themselves. Property was considered indispensable for those seeking a secure niche in the modern division of knowledge labor. It is interesting to note that where land tenure in England was traditionally considered "scarce and valuable,"[12] tenure in America eventually became associated with the guarantee of lifetime employment for academic scholars and was conditioned on the scarcity and value of knowledge as a form of property. Isaiah Berlin characterized real property rights as a form of "negative liberty"; that is, "freedom from interference with one's own choices and projects."[13] One could say much the same thing for academic tenure, which confers a property right. Brian Tamanaha reports that many professors now "demand that they be paid to relinquish" tenure.[14] Knowledge as a form of property was also assumed in the establishment of copyright. Although not reserved just for scholars, a copyright did secure whatever they could produce and get published. Patents, too, were property. Unlike tenure, copyrights and patents "were limited in duration, but there was no doubt that they were property."[15]

The Ascendance of Academe

The growth of professionalism took hold in a rapidly changing and complicated republic, whose population craved knowledge as much as their predecessors had yearned for land. In the late 1800s, many institutions of higher education moved away from their religious and denominational roots to become secular universities prepared to nurture both old and new professions. In addition, newly established universities offered specialized knowledge and services to an expanding economy and a growing urban population. Amateur seekers of enlightenment could now become "professionals" who could apply their expertise in a new, progressive era of government oversight and intervention. Even before American universities emerged in the late nineteenth century with all of their curricular specialties, Charles Eliot, the president of Harvard, in 1869 pointed the way: "As a people, we do not apply to mental activities the principle of the division of labor; and we have but a halting faith in special training for professional employments. The vulgar conceit that a Yankee can turn his hand to anything we insensibly carry into high places, where it is preposterous and criminal . . . This lack of faith in the prophecy of a natural bent, and the value of a discipline concentrated upon a single object, amounts to a national danger."[16] The American university became a place where special fields of knowledge were the proud steeds that each professor sat astride as they sought to educate and train their student charges.

When knowledge treated as a form of property found a home in American higher education, academe grew rapidly and prospered. It developed, in part, through the journeys of approximately ten thousand young American men to German universities, where they acquired training and respect for a system that was far more academic than American higher education at the time. This academic training was detached, highly theoretical work, which offered a status that American students brought back home. In their eyes, America was in need of rigorous, specialized research and scholarship. They had acquired the necessary detachment to shape the idea of secular universities that would no longer be the product of, or beholden to, religious denominations, which had been the curators of traditional American colleges.

A generation before the establishment of what would become the research university model in higher education, legislation in 1862 created the Extension Service, part of newly created state universities where "adoption and diffusion research" was to be shared with a still agricultural-centered America. "Under the cloak of 'scientific objectivity,' land grant research and Extension programming" became an important influence in that agricultural world.[17] Still, it was private universities and their graduate schools, beginning with Johns Hopkins in Baltimore in 1876 followed by the University of Chicago, Columbia, and Stanford, among others, which began to set the bar higher. By and large, the new secular universities established competitive, rather than cooperative, learning environments for their students who were tested on their individual abilities to be independent. American schooling, whether at home or in a schoolhouse, had long sought to develop the self-reliance of young people. The instruction to "do your own work" always served the interests of teachers who had to assign grades and determine which students advanced. The solo performance of the freestanding rational individual in a university classroom prevailed. Consequently, the acquisition of specialized knowledge was largely treated as a prized possession for graduates seeking to be self-reliant and to make a living in an ambitious era.

In academe, a scholar's standing was also "dependent upon admission to and reputation within a community of peers," since knowledge, considered and valued as a form of property, belonged first to an academic discipline or profession.[18] It was not the personal property of those who contributed to its making, revision, and dissemination. It was property held in common by all those who contributed. Those in the know depended on learning from and instructing their peers in an academic give-and-take. The division of mental labor and the proliferation of narrower occupation specialties made such interdependence inevitable. In academia, at least, the originality of someone's contribution was highly valued, sometimes more so than its utility, assuming that whatever paradigm currently prevailed was properly observed. Each academic community offered productive resources for those admitted to its precincts and barred those who lacked the credentials. To those so entitled, specialized knowledge shared with peers offered something valuable, given its scarcity and a demand for it beyond the boundaries of academe. Such scarcity and demand were far different from the abundance of land in America's nineteenth-century expansion. Specialized knowledge was increasingly in demand in a growing urban and industrial America, and professional know-how became a new measure of a man's standing in this fast-changing society. According to Burton Bledstein: "By invoking the highest ideals—talent, merit, achievement—the educational system sanctioned the privileges, indeed the affluence of an accredited individual in American society. Theoretically, neither birth nor prejudice nor favoritism restricted those privileges."[19] It is little wonder then that academe became the "home office" of professionalism. "By and large the American university came into existence to serve and promote professional authority in society . . . [making] possible a social faith in merit, competencies, discipline, and control that were basic to accepted conceptions of achievement and success."[20]

At the heart of this shift in professional priorities was the Germanic precedent of academic freedom for the detached scholar combined with the ambitions of higher education institutions to reach out for more professional properties, which they saw as ripe intellectual territory to add to the growing estate of their graduate schools. A useful analogy is the 1930 naming of the constellations by the International Astronomical Union, given the pace of celestial discoveries in the twentieth century. Consequently, astronomers established an official set of constellation boundaries. So, too, the ascendance of academe called for establishing the boundaries and naming the many "knowledge constellations" within its system. Soon the American university cast its shadow over a wide range of professionalized occupations with "quasi-academic specialization of focus . . . mimicking academic habits of thought."[21]

Before this new era of academe, professional schools had been mostly proprietary and admission was fairly easily attained. The schools of medicine and law, which once had been independent entities, came into the fold, as well as teacher-training schools and schools of engineering and business. The number of professional schools grew at a remarkable pace. Medical schools more than doubled.[22] Law schools grew from 28 with 600 students in 1870 to 100 schools with 13,000 students in 1900.[23] At Harvard Law School, Dean Langdell redefined the law as a "science" not fit for apprenticeship.[24] Overall the number of professional schools doubled in the period from 1876 to 1900.[25] Rational inquiry and empirical evidence fast became the standard for "modern" professionals. In 1870 there were 563 institutions with 5,553 faculty members. By 1900 there were 977 such institutions, with 23,968 faculty. The number of students who received bachelor degrees doubled in that same thirty-year period.[26]

American colleges had once sought to educate "public" men for leadership in a growing republic, but American universities and their graduate schools soon pursued a different path. The turning point came in the 1890s when graduate school faculty priorities "shifted from that of preparing men for public life and toward that of reproducing their own academic selves."[27] Although the mission was to educate for professional employment and offer credentials that might possibly become a license for government service, this was not academe's main purpose. Academics labored for the approval of their peers, not for the sake of the public, and their example was a lesson for would-be professional students—professional authority is *conferred* by peers, not *earned* with the public.[28] Nothing could capture this more pointedly than Talcott Parsons in 1939, then a leading American sociologist, who argued that sociology as a "scientific discipline" was "clearly dedicated to the advancement and transmission of empirical knowledge" and only "secondarily to the communication of such knowledge to non-members."[29]

Even today, some academics see "politics" and "power" in every text and institution, and nonetheless, pursue their critiques in orthodox academic fashion. They deconstruct but rarely communicate with the larger public. There are rewards for their academic performance but their efforts rarely benefit the real world constituencies that inspire their scholarship. Henry Rosovsky, former dean and professor emeritus at Harvard, wrote: "The essence of academic life is the opportunity—indeed—the demand for continued investment in oneself."[30] An emeritus professor of American studies offered this: "Postmodernism has become so institutionalized and so conventional, so deeply embedded into the academic meritocracy" that, when he argued that postmodernism was "fundamentally anti-democratic," he encountered some very critical commentary.[31]

With the ascendance of academe, academic associations emerged in areas such as modern language, American history, and mathematics, culminating in the Association of University Professors. These professional organizations helped to secure the recently asserted academic freedom of graduate school and faculty members.[32] The development of national standards for the accreditation of graduate schools arose not as a state function but as a means of offering evaluative benchmarks for those seeking reassurance that a university and its programs were meeting established standards. Regional accreditation agencies as private organizations served the interests of institutions of higher education seeking confirmation from disinterested outsiders who were academic professionals themselves. Accreditation was tied to state licensing to the extent that graduates of unaccredited schools or programs could be barred from obtaining professional licenses. And with such academic organizing also came tenure, which meant lifelong employment, in most cases for academics who for years had been subject to the whims of administrators or the political biases of trustees. What constituted a professor's independence? Samuel Haber, professor emeritus at University of California, Berkeley, observed: "His independence did not mean complete freedom from external control but rather that the most essential commands that he obeyed he himself should give. The justification for giving those commands would not come from his own will or from the organization of which he was a part, but from exalted values beyond the reach of both."[33]

Beyond academe, professional guilds emerged, each sharing a common language, concepts, and established boundaries that other guilds respected. Certain professions also secured the support of state licensing, thus creating a monopoly of practice with credential requirements. As described by Albert W. Dzur, a political science and philosophy professor,

"Licensing is the paragon of self-regulation: it excludes laypeople from performing certain tasks or roles and gives fellow professionals pride of place as gatekeepers."[34] Licensing can be compared to conveying a deed that gives greater security to a property owner. The worthy purpose of licensing was to protect the public from incompetence and quackery; however, licensing "also worked to restrict the number of practitioners, thereby raising their incomes."[35] The professional establishment became far removed from the delicensing trend in the Jacksonian era of the early to mid-nineteenth century. "When institutionalized credentials and professions began their comeback at the end of the century their advocates could justify them . . . by their potential contribution to national economic progress. This was arguing the case for professions on terms Jacksonians would understand, if not always accept."[36]

Credentialed, specialized knowledge thus was treated as a form of property secured by the ascent of the American university and all that followed from academe's strategic positioning in a rapidly changing society. Like owners of real property, academics and practicing professionals began to take for granted that they could exclude others from such ownership without being accountable to anyone but their peers. Their property was firmly secured and maintained by academic departments, graduate schools, professional associations, licensing, and codes. In many cases, professions had statutory standing that reinforced their special, societal roles—for example, lawyers, doctors, and members of the press. Although specialization is not synonymous with the professions and can be practiced in any skilled trade, as more and more professions made their home in the growing estate of the American university, academe's influence grew. According to Bender and Schorske, "between 1940 and 1990, federal funds for higher education increased by a factor of twenty-five, enrollment by ten, and average teaching loads were reduced by half."[37]

In the twentieth century the culture of professionalism, which had rejected earlier forms of external authority, relocated its own "authority" in the modern university and various academic precincts. There were, however, some hiccups along the way. In the 1960s and 1970s a number of critics (Ivan Illich, Randall Collins, Burton Bledstein, John McKnight, and Theodore Roszak, to name a few) chronicled or protested the professional takeover of public life. And there were Baby Boomers who, as college students, challenged Clark Kerr's "multiuniversity" concept when he served as president at the University of California at Berkeley. The free speech movement on Berkeley's campus declared "do not fold, spindle or mutilate" using punch cards as a metaphor for their alienation from and denunciation of the multiuniversity"—its bureaucracy and central cultural role. The Boomer generation defied "the system," but did not give much thought to what should take its place; so the great majority made their peace with the status quo and found a place in the established order. This may have been a rather detached and cynical adjustment that might explain why so many became so-called "yuppies" (young urban professionals) putting some distance between them and the institutions they once discredited. As newly minted professionals, it also separated them from those who had no credentials. Many Baby Boomers never did reconcile the contradiction between wanting to get ahead and not leaving anyone behind.

Social historian Laurence Veysey made the astute comment that the American university "thrives on ignorance" thereby creating the conditions for "a diverse but fundamentally stable organization."[38] Each specialist has a niche whose status depends on a modicum of deference among his or her peers. Such are the self-imposed limits that most professionals observe—a "golden rule" of deferring unto other credentialed specialists as you would have them defer unto you. So when a new niche in academia seeks recognition as a would-be program or department, there is often resistance, but more often there is acceptance as long as the change does not usurp anyone else's position. Gerald Graff observed: "When a threatening innovation appeared—modernist literature, the New Criticism, avant-garde art, Marxist economics, creative writing, econometrics, psychohistory, feminism, or deconstruction—its proponents, after an initial period of struggle, could be appeased by the addition of a new course, program, or department to the aggregate. But the traditionalists who opposed the innovation were also appeased since they did not have to alter their own practices or engage in serious debate with the newcomers."[39] The golden rule of deference in the culture of professionalism keeps the peace but also seriously restrains those who might otherwise trespass for good reason.

Academe is far from settled. The increasing use of adjuncts is undermining the prize of tenure, which many academics no longer can expect. As one professor told me, "the [economics] of the current system puts so much strain on the tenure culture that I'm not sure we can ever find a fulcrum between the haves and the have-nots."[40] Another professor told me of the increasing importance of "the goals and aspirations of the 'new faculty majority,' the two-thirds (more, by some counts) of college and university faculty working off the tenure track as contract or contingent instructors. This large group of colleagues is defined explicitly as 'not scholars' or 'not researchers' by virtue of being defined as 'exclusively teachers.'" She added that in just a few years "the galaxy of tenure-track and tenured faculty" has shrunk "radically, relative to that of contract faculty."[41]

The focus of professional practice beyond the ivory tower is on the *marketability* of whatever knowledge is produced. This is increasingly the case within academe as research becomes more commercialized and knowledge is treated as "proprietary" rather than as something to be freely disseminated.[42] Consequently, as "universities openly and increasingly pursue commercialization . . . [they] function openly and enthusiastically as entrepreneurial, competitive, profit-making corporations."[43] One academic told me she resents and fears

> those who want to privatize and corporatize education, put it in the service of the for-profit sector via job training, and basically undo all of education that is, precisely, not immediately useful in a market-driven world . . . [T]he liberal arts and sciences are under very serious attack in ways that threaten freedom of thought, speculation, research in favor of a utilitarian reduction, and particularly to job training for the for-profit sector. I find myself muttering these days that I worry about a civilization that cannot find reason to support "useless" efforts to conserve past traditions and great works; critical, independent thinking; "pure" research that interests the best minds. . . teaching that practices independent thinking; any activity that is not market-driven.[44]

Those who are ensnared in academe confront some brutal facts: Soaring tuitions are leading many into serious debt for credentials that no longer guarantee a job (currently, there is more than $1 trillion in student debt overall with seven million student loan borrowers in default); law school applications are at a thirty-year low and enrollment in other graduate programs are in serious decline; almost half of undergraduates are failing to earn a degree within six years; and there is a significant decline in government support for public colleges and universities.

The Socialization of Would-Be Professionals

The socialization of would-be professionals is a critical passage and cornerstone of America's culture of professionalism. Socialization in the academic setting is a process by which a student comes to adopt the values and attitudes of the culture. It can begin at the undergraduate level with the frequent use of textbooks that offer a distorted picture of how knowledge is actually shaped. In textbooks, knowledge is presented as a "done deal" for the student to admire and absorb. Such tidy packaging obscures the trial-and-error process in which real learning and knowledge creation is grounded. Consequently, scientific research can be seriously misconstrued in textbooks. There is a substantial difference "between textbooks of scientific method and the ways in which scientists actually think, feel, and go about their work."[45] Thomas Kuhn put it another way—"the textbook tendency to make the development of science linear hides a process that lies at the heart of the most significant episodes of scientific development."[46] And Robert Merton noted: "The books on methods present ideal patterns, but these tidy, normative patterns . . . do not reproduce the typically untidy, opportunistic adaptations that scientists really make."[47] Duncan Watts argues: "Doing science is really a lot like doing anything else, but by the time it gets out into the larger social world and everyone reads about it in books, it has been so reworked and refined that it takes on an aura of inevitability it never had in the making." Watts notes that "real science occurs in the same messy ambiguous world that scientists struggle to clarify, and is done by real people who suffer the same kind of limitations and confusions as anybody else."[48] Nonetheless, textbook learning is considered a useful shortcut as students eventually become willing tenants of the academic landlords who preside. Those not seeking to be scholars harvest what knowledge they can, hoping it is what they need to secure a job and make a good living.[49]

One thing is certain: at the present time a great majority of students socialized in academe remain fixed in doing whatever it takes to get the credentials they think they need to succeed in America's culture of professionalism. In many colleges and universities this consumer model resembles a department store earnestly catering to every taste and need. As a result, some institutions offer little or no educational vision of their own. Symptomatic of academe's consumer model, PayScale.com has introduced a new metric of postgraduate salaries. It ranks more than a thousand colleges and universities "by the average earnings of their graduates." Given the soaring costs and associated debt burdens imposed on students, this is an appropriate but very limited measure of what academe potentially offers.[50] It is conceivable, however, that even graduates armed with credentials will gain less than they expected. Fred Hirsch, a professor of International Studies, developed the depressing but logical scenario that in a "positional economy" competition for place has "everyone standing on tiptoe" with the ludicrous result that everyone will end up in the same position as where they started. That does not bode well for the culture of professionalism that thrives on status differences. Hirsch argues that the competition for place runs into unavoidable "social scarcity."[51]

For those seeking to be scholars and teachers, graduate school socialization is more important and lasting. "Students move from being readers and consumers . . . to being producers of knowledge."[52] Would-be professionals are there to learn the paradigms of the professors' respective jurisdictions and rarely question the work habits that accompany such learning. Following the example of those who teach them, students pursue not only *what* they should learn but *how* they should learn it. David Damrosch, a critic of the existing culture in academe, points out that the "tolerance for solitary work," which diminishes "intellectual sociability," reduces the "ability to address problems that require collaborative solutions."[53] Such a learning experience can also be a form of indoctrination. A seasoned academic expressed her concern to me that graduate students "are socialized into the self-protective, irresponsible notion that knowledge comes from elsewhere than a shareable world, and has no consequences, thence no responsibility to such a world, and others."[54] Those who share personal anecdotes soon learn that such offerings have little or no value in some fields. The abstract can also be suspect as the historian Thomas Haskell recalls with his own personal anecdote:

> During a visit many years ago to Princeton's Davis Center Seminar, when a paper of mine was criticized because it was not pitched at the matter-of-fact level that historians take to be natural, I was so bold as to shrug and suggest that from the standpoint of the profession I might well be a "recruiting error." The center's director and its senior members stiffened in stony silence, taking my words to be a gauche confession of personal delinquency, too embarrassing to be uttered in public. The graduate students, not yet fully socialized, understood that it was no confession and laughed uproariously.[55]

Charles Lindblom recalled his indoctrination into the field of economics: "The impact of my early years in graduate training was, as for many of my colleagues, a seductive influence from which I can never wholly recover."[56] Nonetheless, it was Lindblom who spent much of his academic life casting a skeptical eye on his economics profession challenging its scientific and static tendencies.

Although teaching is often why graduate students pursue a career in academe, their elders' preoccupation with research often turns them away from why they came to graduate school in the first place.[57] With another perspective, a female professor told me: "I think the fundamental lesson of graduate school, aside from cognitive development, is learning to be humble and what humility means for an academic . . . Basically graduate school is run in an apprenticeship fashion . . . working on papers as a team, presenting at conferences, and then submitting for publication. Ultimately, I think the whole process of review and publication does have the goal of producing knowledge but also keeping you humble."[58] A colleague with a doctorate in public administration took a different view of graduate school "socialization": "Tragically, the models of indoctrination are too often those who are the most skilled [in] mastering a narrow swath of knowledge that often governs the field. Whereas we often hear these wonderful anecdotes about the great prof who made us think, that person is seldom the one who is the model for indoctrination."[59] An emeritus professor objected to the example set by some of his colleagues and told me: "When I directed the American Studies graduate program, I admitted a marginal student because he had a real voice, and I was drawn to that authenticity. Sadly, when I read a couple of years later his written exams or field proposals . . . he sounded like everyone else: big and pretentious and smart and completely voiceless. All that reading and theory had robbed him of his voice. Very sad and troubling."[60] The same emeritus professor also shared this:

> I took part in designing a certificate of civic engagement for graduate students from across the colleges and disciplines . . . My first graduate assistant . . . came from the English department. She came to me in tears one day, confessing she was scared to death about the job market, that she had no nibbles for teaching positions, etc. I encouraged her to think about alternative careers and talked to her about it in positive ways, and invited her to keep up the conversation with me. She had had no counseling or personal advice from faculty in her department . . . No one had given her permission to think in different ways about career. Not a peep from her

professors. Long story short: she now works for a labor union in NYC, and she is flourishing. An "ecology" requires a diverse pool of possibilities to flourish, not a single track or puddle.[61]

Some of those pursuing careers in academia by mastering a narrow swath of knowledge are likely to become what Clifford Geertz calls (borrowing from Isaiah Berlin's oft-used metaphor) "hypothesis hedgehogs." By contrast, using Geertz's terms again, the would-be professionals who leave academia will of necessity become "fieldwork foxes."[62] Hedgehogs tend to one crop while foxes roam across many fields. As a practicing lawyer I learned, as Geertz put it, that "legal facts are . . . socially constructed."[63] So what I learned during law school was only the beginning of my education. Much knowledge can only be acquired through experience and observation of specific situations—what Geertz would describe as "orienting notions, not foundational ones."[64] Those who become salaried professionals are also likely to be "fieldwork foxes." They rarely have the standing or autonomy of professionals with their own practices and enterprises. Harold Wilensky noted that "the salaried professional often has neither exclusive or final responsibility for his work; he must accept the ultimate authority of non-professionals in the assessment of both process and product." However, "the crux of the issue of autonomy for salaried professionals is whether the organization itself is infused with professionalism."[65] The particular culture then of an organization is a critical dimension for salaried professionals. There are "custodians" who are often unofficial representatives of what an organization values. If such custodians are professionally minded, more than likely the organization will be as well.

The Ice Cream Factory (I)

The Ice Cream Factory had been built in what had once been cornfields. An interstate highway separated the factory from the old town. Gleaming white buildings with green glass windows is all that Dewey could see. The factory had devoured the cornfields for miles in either direction running parallel to the Interstate. No trees or shrubbery broke the horizontal plane.

Dewey stood in the shadow of the Interstate's concrete arch. The viaduct provided a view of the factory grounds. Shielding his eyes, Dewey looked up and down at the bright white building of this new world at the edge of town. Just where would he work, in which building would he live, through which door should he enter? He looked back at the old town with its familiar clutter of peaked roofs, church spires, and sooted chimneys. There was no future there; he knew that. Dewey had no choice. He stared at his shoes. If you wanted work, you went to the Ice Cream Factory. There was no other job in town for an ambitious young man. He turned again toward the factory. Somewhere in that sprawling encampment was Dewey's new home.

Dewey set out for Building #109 which stood closest to the Interstate viaduct. Through a revolving door of green glass, he entered a large lobby of what appeared to be white marble. In the center of the lobby behind a white lacquered table sat a guard or someone Dewey thought looked like a guard. The man was dressed in a white uniform except for a Sam Browne belt on which a metal coin changer was attached.

"May I help you?" the guard inquired.

"I'm looking for a job," Dewey replied. "Am I in the right building? There are so many."

"Please sign the register and I will tell you."

Dewey signed his name in a large book open in the center of the white lacquered table.

"Dewey is it? Dewey, you are now in Building #109. There is a personnel office here and there is a personnel office in every building of the Ice Cream Factory."

"Which one should I go to?"

"That's entirely up to you," the guard replied.

"You mean I can work in any building that I want to?"

The guard nodded, "assuming that you agree to the factory manager's conditions. I'll take you to the personnel officer here in Building #109. You will be speaking with our Mr. Dasher."

Dewey followed the guard down a long hallway. The white walls and white carpet made it seem like a tunnel of snow unrelieved by any feature or color until they entered a small windowless room.

There, every color decorated the walls, the ceiling, and the floor. Dewey imagined that he had passed through a white shaft into a kaleidoscope. He had difficulty locating the voice that greeted him.

"Another job applicant, Fussell?"

"Yes, Mr. Dasher. His name is Dewey." The guard apparently named Fussell gave a smart salute and left Dewey to his interview.

"Sit down young man." Dewey located the voice in the corner where an orange metal desk was set diagonally at the intersection of pink and red walls. From behind the desk peered a small pinched face, pale and aged with yellowish white hair falling to rounded shoulders. Mr. Dasher looked at Dewey through large tinted glasses. His mouth had the slack look of someone who had tired of his job long ago.

"Can you find a chair? There, that blue one is close enough. Sit down, Dewey."

Mr. Dasher had not offered a handshake and Dewey did as he was directed. He sat in the blue painted chair against the wall and shifted slightly to face Mr. Dasher.

"Too much color for you, Dewey? I suppose it's the factory manager's idea—a reminder of all the flavors that The Factory makes. I can't stand so many colors. I wear these glasses instead—makes everything look green."

"Oh," is all that Dewey could say.

"My old section," Dasher went on, "was Lime Sherbert where I worked for twenty years before someone made me an ad-min-is-tra-tor." Mr. Dasher drew the word out with a weary resignation. Then with a little cackle, he started drumming his fingers on the orange desktop. Dewey had never seen anyone drum their fingers so fast, and what was more curious, Dasher drummed with both hands.

"I suppose it would be nice to have windows—to have something else to look at," Dewey offered.

"Windows? No one in the Factory has windows." Dasher lifted his tinted glasses and stared at Dewey.

"But I saw green glass windows in every building—stretching for miles," as Dewey motioned to what he thought were the outside walls of the personnel office.

Mr. Dasher started drumming on the desktop again. "I'm telling you, young man, that no one who works in the Ice Cream Factory has windows."

Dewey changed the subject. "Fussell, as you call him . . . "

"Fussell is his name!" Mr. Dasher interrupted. "All the former Good Humor men work as guards now in the Ice Cream Factory." Mr. Dasher blew his nose into a very large purple handkerchief.

Dewey continued. "Well, Fussell said I could go to any personnel office in any building, so he brought me to you. I want a job."

"Everyone does who comes here," Dasher cackled. "We never turn anyone away. You can be black, brown, white, yellow, lime sherbert—makes no difference to the factory manager as long as you accept the conditions. The Ice Cream Factory is an equal opportunity employer," Mr. Dasher interrupted himself. "Fussell, oh, did Fussell tell you about the conditions?"

"No sir," Dewey replied.

"Good, that is my business to tell you. His business is to tell you that. Did he?" The fingers started drumming.

"Did he tell me?" Dewey tried to find the answer that Mr. Dasher wanted. "Fussell didn't tell me anything about conditions. That's your business."

"Good for Fussell." Mr. Dasher looked pleased. "The conditions are very simple, Dewey. Anyone could explain them to you." Dasher paused and blew his nose again. "If you want to work at the Ice Cream Factory, you have to choose a flavor. All your training will be in one flavor. You learn about making ice cream by learning how to make a flavor. You will agree that ice cream without flavor is mean-ing-less." Dasher rested on the last word as if it were to be put away in a desk drawer or lost in a shirt pocket—forever. "Well, Dewey, what flavor will it be?"

Dewey didn't have the slightest idea what to say. He shifted his chair and stared at his shoes.

"We make 457 flavors," said Dasher. "Let me check the morning bulletin to be sure." Mr. Dasher looked in the direction of his in-box. "No, it's 459 as of this morning. That doesn't count how many flavors that are in development—not certified yet by the steering committee.

When I came here, Dewey, there were 114 and I chose Lime Sherbert. A young man like you now has four times as many flavors to choose from." Again glancing at what apparently was the morning bulletin, Dasher announced—"Two more flavors certified just yesterday by the steering committee—Candy Cotton and Guava Bisque."

Dewey tried to think. It was an important decision. Mr. Dasher had been in Lime Sherbert for twenty years. "May I see the list?"

Dasher had anticipated the question and was opening a large book holding computer printout sheets. "Take a look. They are all here—all certified." Dewey pulled his chair over and faced Dasher across the orange desktop. He looked at the printouts. He never knew that there were so many flavors.

"Dewey, don't make it a big problem. The Factory makes ice cream. Ice cream is good, so all flavors are equally good. Do you agree?

"That seems reasonable," said Dewey.

"It is not only reasonable. It is a condition of working here that you agree that all flavors are good. The factory manager will have it no other way." Dasher's fingers started drumming on the printout sheet that Dewey was staring at.

"So it doesn't matter which flavor that I choose? Is that right, Mr. Dasher?"

"You're catching on, Dewey," Dasher offered gently as he closed the large book. "They need some help in Butter Almond. Why don't you sign up? Of course, I can't tell what you'll be doing for them— that is up to their society. Each flavor has a society that takes you in and puts you to work. So, Dewey, will it be Butter Almond?"

Dewey looked at Mr. Dasher and then at his shoes. If he said "No, I want to try Black Raspberry," what would this little man, hunched behind the desk, do? If all flavors were good, on what basis could Dewey decline Dasher's recommendation of Butter Almond? Dewey wanted to get along. Dewey wanted a job. He would learn to adjust. "Butter Almond sounds fine to me, Mr. Dasher."

"Good, Dewey. You obviously understand the conditions."

Dewey was pleased with himself. Dasher started to scribble a note that Dewey thought was probably an introduction to the Butter

Almond Society. "I should tell you, Mr. Dasher, that I already know a bit about making ice cream. My mother made it at home for my sister and me."

Dasher looked up at Dewey. His eyes were hidden again behind the tinted glasses, but his mouth pursed with a little sour expression. The fingers stopped writing and started drumming. "I must tell you, young man, that you didn't learn anything from your mother that will help you here."

Dewey was sorry that he had offered his little boast. He wanted Mr. Dasher to finish whatever he was writing.

"I'm only a personnel officer. But on behalf of the Ice Cream Factory and with all due respect to your mother, she can't possibly know how to make ice cream—not the kind that is made here."

Dewey was as offended by Dasher's remark as Dasher seemed to be by Dewey's comment about homemade ice cream. But Dewey let it pass. He was grateful to have a job. There really was no other place to work for someone with ambition like himself. Dasher had resumed his writing and Dewey waited for the contract, or so the document seemed to be—signed, sealed, and delivered into his sweating hands.

"There," said Dasher, "you take this to Butter Almond in Building #75. And on your way, ask Fussell to give you a tour of the factory. You will be too busy to see much of it later. Well, good luck, Dewey." Dasher rose from his chair and all but shouted— "Don't expect an office with a window, Dew-ey." Dasher cackled and plunged his nose into the purple handkerchief.

Dewey knew that the interview was over, mumbled his thanks, and reentered the white hallway in search of Fussell and Building #75.

CHAPTER 2

"Thriving on Ignorance"

L aurence Veysey, who saw the irony of universities thriving on ignorance, observed that "the patterned isolation of [their] component parts . . . required that people continually talk past each other . . . This lack of comprehension, which safeguards one's privacy and one's illusions, doubtless occurs in many groups, but it may be of special importance in explaining the otherwise unfathomable behavior of society's most intelligent members."[1] With the coming of expertise, John Dewey claimed, "Man has never had such a varied body of knowledge in his possession before."[2] But Dewey's "man" was an abstraction—he didn't exist. He never will. Thomas Sowell made the distinction that "the intellectual advantage" of civilized man over the primitive savage is not that "he has more knowledge, but that he requires far less."[3] And that is why the coming of credentialed expertise has flourished and compensated for everyone's ignorance about most things.

Adam Smith's analysis of why productivity increases under the division of manual labor can also be applied to the division of mental labor. According to Smith, the division of manual labor improves each worker's dexterity through specialization and saves time by not having the worker move from one kind of job to another.[4] The advance of knowledge was spectacular for the very reason that its pursuit was organized without the ambition that anyone could possess all that was to be found. The spectacular productivity, however, resulting from the division of mental labor cannot be fully accounted for by Smith's rationale for the division of manual labor. Equally important is the unfettered pursuit of "truth"— an open-ended process, an infinite trail that natural and social scientists forged or followed, constantly replacing "truths" known with new "truths" discovered. Unlike the rejects of Smith's assembly line, which were cast aside and never reached the market, error was assumed and tolerated in the production of knowledge—not because such knowledge was carelessly produced but because error was a necessary part of perfecting what was already known.

And so fledgling American universities undertook the division of mental labor in order to better serve an emerging urban and industrial society. In doing so, the secular university freed itself from the religious constraints of the sectarian college. The priority became the pursuit of specialized knowledge—not moral instruction—to promote and accommodate economic and social change. The division of mental labor was a pragmatic response to an increasingly ambitious and complicated society. It spawned new academic disciplines, new university departments, and new professions—each producing an abundance of new knowledge and an abundance of specialists. By 1900 approximately 3,500 doctorates had been granted at a rate of about 500 per year. By 1960 there were 10,000 doctorates being awarded annually in 550 fields of scholarship. By 2000, approximately 60,000 were awarded each year.[5]

In our current knowledge society, everyone, including credentialed experts, lives in a state of unavoidable ignorance of the knowledge that is produced across academic disciplines. There is little chance an expert even within a particular field can master its entire body of continually growing and changing hypotheses and findings. Experts really have little choice but to operate with their minds in a groove.[6] Social scientist Donald Schon argued that the scope of expertise is also "limited by situations of uncertainty, instability, uniqueness, and conflict. When research-based theories and techniques are inapplicable, the professional cannot legitimately claim to be an expert."[7]

It is beyond organizations, including universities, to fully grasp the respective contributions of their experts. Talcott Parsons put it in more positive terms: "members are expected to follow a tolerant 'live and let live' policy in their mutual relations, respecting the spheres in which others claim special competence and interest."[8] And so Veysey was right to say that institutions in academe thrive on ignorance. As a consequence, "knowledge has been accumulated, [and] the individual teacher or researcher has gained an additional dimension of freedom, which flows from so specialized an understanding of a particular area of knowledge as to make impracticable or impossible the direction or control of his activities by others."[9] In exchange for such autonomy, "experts" are expected "to ask important questions, to competently conduct research, to assess others' work, to understand the important ideas of their field, to communicate what they know, and to apply their knowledge and understanding to solve important problems."[10] The question is, do they?

Making Assumptions

Veysey's reference to "illusions" in academe is intriguing and worth exploring. According to *The American Heritage College Dictionary* (Fourth Edition), an illusion" is an "erroneous perception of reality," a misconception, a confusion—a kind of ignorance. Assumptions, predictions, and "hold still" modeling are standard equipment in many academic toolkits but, when limiting the number of variables, each may qualify as an "illusion." The division of mental labor allows various academic disciplines, within their respective knowledge properties, to take for granted assumptions that may be serious misconceptions of how things work in the real world. Assumptions in academe are not just captured in each discipline's worldview. There is also the assumption, or perhaps constant expectation, that scholars will attend to producing new knowledge. Unfortunately, the emphasis on producing *new* knowledge sometimes has the consequence of originality trumping utility. When a discipline has its own hypothesis for human behavior, it can sometimes turn out to be "more wishful gospel than empirical truth."[11] Furthermore, taking for granted the basic assumptions within an academic discipline can come to rule an undergraduate classroom where such assumptions are often ingested and used without critical examination. And for "novice researchers" in doctoral programs "all scholarship emerges from a set of assumptions about the nature of the world, reality, and . . . such assumptions influence the ways in which research is conceptualized, operationalized, and evaluated—though these beliefs are often left unexplored and unspoken."[12] Students, undergraduate or graduate, may very well be led to believe that established assumptions have a permanent place in their learning. Nonetheless, a dynamic, ever-changing real world challenges many unexamined classroom assumptions. As John Dewey noted, "that which is taught is thought of as essentially static. It is taught as a finished product . . . and yet it is used as educational food in a society where change is the rule, not the exception."[13] For Dewey then, and in academe now, "inculcation of fixed conclusions rather than the development of intelligence as a method of action still dominates [education's] processes."[14]

Consider the rational choice model in the field of economics. The model's assumptions, which once prevailed but are now seriously contested within economics, illustrate how knowledge and ignorance are not that far removed from each other when professionals establish and rely on assumptions that are not in accord with the real world. The assumption that a rational individual's self-interest is unalterable often does not jibe with actual experience or restrain an individual from entertaining preferences beyond his self-interest. Psychologist Barry Schwartz argued: "Rational economic man as a reflection of human nature is a fiction."[15] For example, game theory, the study of rational expectations in interdependent situations, usually models "players" without individual identities or a social context in which their choices are made. Game theory is centered on the thinking realm of individual "players" who engage each other, rather than the behavioral realm in which social relationships represent a different and often unpredictable dimension. Individual self-interest, which a game theorist assumes is inherent and unvarying in every "player," may not adequately account for behavior learned through social interaction. Game theory, by and large, ignores the complexity of individual motivation in the real world. It assumes, as does much of economic theory, that "players" are totally rational, pursuing their respective self-interests. Like all models, it simplifies the important dynamics of competition, conflict, and cooperation, and can be unreliable in predicting an actual player's behavior in a given context. Game theory's assumptions and modeling make it an interesting method for predicting or producing actual outcomes, but it is entirely too abstract. It ignores the real world contexts in which interdependent choices are made. Nonetheless, even though any context contains a host of variables, game theorists find it difficult to incorporate many in their model. Such variables may include the norms and precedents of how a "game" is played in a particular venue—such as business negotiations or contested divorce proceedings—or the players' respective identities, roles and reputations, and the likely inconsistency of their preferences if the "game" has successive rounds and develops its own unique narrative. Organizational sociologist Mary Zey is right: "Organizational decision makers do not make context-independent decisions because their existence is context dependent."[16]

Behavioral economics challenges the assumption that rational man behaves predictably in the real world. Instead, he often entertains preferences beyond his self-interest and may even know how best to advance his self-interest. In his study on expertise, Philip Tetlock found that faulty assumptions were compounded by the temptation to be less critical of one's own assumptions and more critical of assumptions that challenged whatever projections have been made.[17] My former colleague Gerry Brewer argued: "Organizations frequently leave out the very assumptions that are most important or most threatening to their sense of themselves."[18] Michael Schrage, at MIT's Media Lab, says that such an argument is why Brewer "believes so strongly that unexplored assumptions can reveal more than those assumptions that are articulated."[19]

I asked several academics whether the working assumptions of their respective disciplines deserve reconsideration. They provided a variety of responses. One individual told me that "a full industry of academic periodicals" is "the primary focus" of many of his faculty colleagues, but such a focus for him is "simply too narrow." Each discipline has developed its own set of journals, and "faculty can publish in those journals without having to make sense to anyone outside their discipline. It's actually even worse now, because each discipline has its own sub-disciplines now, so the whole process is bifurcating even more."[20] Another academic put it more forcefully: "theoretical cat cradles, and being smart as hell are markers of status . . . And we somehow need to debunk smarties from a mindset that views critical assaults on theory as evidence of bad faith anti-intellectualism."[21] And there was this interesting response from an associate professor of higher education: "The assumption that the dissertation, as it is currently conducted . . . is the best way to (a) make a distinct contribution to knowledge [and] (b) demonstrate mastery of a topic—needs to be reconsidered."[22] An academic in the humanities told me she is drawn to interdisciplinary studies, which have the merit that "since one is never fully immersed in any one discipline . . . the expertise or insider knowledge associated with immersion in one discipline is never assumed." She went on: "In my interdisciplinary field, where art and philosophy meet, the focus is always on the questions, rather than providing a single reliable answer. Instead, various approaches and answers are considered, and the way forward is often negotiated through pathways of possibilities rather than a predetermined and linear route."[23] Philosopher Elizabeth Minnich told me that her father Andrew Kamarch, an economist, warned of confusing precision with accuracy. Minnich argues: "The problem is when any one mode of study is taken to be more than it is, as models have in some arenas. Reality . . . always exceeds our efforts to study it, and we do well to remember that . . . we do use our studies . . . to force reality to prove our perforce narrow versions of it."[24] Minnich also offered a telling case about ruling assumptions:

> I was once in a discussion with professors from several fields who were interested in developing a women's studies PhD in their own field. As we proceeded, it became glaringly evident that the few graduate students there literally could only hear what professors said if they, the professors, "spoke postmodern." I confess I found that appalling, but clearly the graduate students were in worlds in which there was one language that indicated brilliance, and had therefore not learned or had erased others. This is not learning to think; this is learning how to get on a moving train and make your way up to the first car.[25]

Making Predictions and "Hold Still" Modeling

Philosopher Karl Popper argued: "Long-term prophesies can be derived from scientific conditional predictions only if they apply to systems which can be described as well-isolated, stationary, and recurrent. These systems are very rare in nature; and modern society is not one of them."[26] Whether in game theory or economic forecasts, predicting future behavior and outcomes is more art than science, regardless of the esoteric methods used. Seeking relative certainty about the future has to be one of the greater conceits of "experts." Nate Silver points out in his excellent study on predictions that most economic forecasters failed to "predict" recessions even when they were underway.[27] Mathematic professors Edward Burger and Michael Starbird point out that "even mathematics, complete and precise, is subject to the perils of tiny variations in initial conditions, which, when multiplied and magnified by the tyrant of repeated application, end by leading us far astray."[28] No doubt, failed attempts to remove uncertainty about the future can reflect badly on the reputations of those who are supposedly smart enough and have enough expertise to overcome such an obstacle. Silver, however, argues: "[E]xperts either aren't very good at providing an honest description of the uncertainty in their forecasts, or they aren't very interested in doing so."[29] At the heart of such failure are the mistaken assumptions made again and again that shape prediction. One assumption that often gets forecasters in trouble is that a "current trend will continue indefinitely into the future."[30] Nate Silver offers the example of what turned out to be the Great Recession, when the Survey of Professional Forecasters opined that "there was less than a 1 in 500 chance that the economy would crash as badly as it did."[31] Silver goes on to note that "overconfident predictions can be found in many other fields, such as medical research, political science, finance and psychology.[32] Philip Tetlock, in his study of expertise, reached an even harsher conclusion: "It didn't matter whether the experts were making predictions about economics, domestic political, or international affairs, their judgment was equally bad across the board."[33] Scott Page, a leader in the study of complex systems, adds: "In making predictions, experts rely on a few dimensions at most. They omit variables that matter, and they sometimes include variables that do not."[34] Bent Flyvbjerg, a professor of planning in Denmark, argues that social inquiry fails when using "predictive theories and universals," and what is needed is "context-dependent knowledge."[35] Nate Silver agrees that context dependency makes prediction a "shared enterprise" and not just "a function that a select group of experts or practitioners perform."[36] That is why the actual experience of nonexperts on the ground, so to speak, is of considerable importance.

Many situations that academic experts seek to investigate are far from static, but researchers often prefer to make reality hold still in order to explain it. Any mutations are seen as exceptions to a static rule. This leads to what I call the "hold still" mentality of researchers who model what are exceedingly complicated and dynamic phenomena. Not wanting to overwhelm a model with too many variables, and not being able to identify variables that may arise at some future time, "hold still" models focus on a limited number of known variables assuming they are sufficient to provide useful projections on which others can depend. James C. Scott, professor of political science and anthropology at Yale, notes that the isolation of "a few variables while assuming everything else constant and the bracketing of interaction effects that lie outside the experimental model are very definitely inscribed in scientific method."[37] That is why economist Paul Krugman notes: "Modeling has the effect of destroying knowledge as well as creating it."[38] There have been times when urban planners in America have attempted to determine planned futures for cities and neighborhoods with hold still modeling that ignored the dynamics of city life. Without isolated and recurrent conditions as preconditions, planners have little chance of securing what they want or think is best, especially in cases where political power is beyond their reach. And even when those with power give planners adequate license and support, even the best laid plans can go awry. People in positions of power have learned that the machinations of planners face many obstacles and unforeseen events. As Philip Tetlock found in his study of expert political judgment: "On the big questions, we could do as well tossing a coin as by consulting accredited experts."[39]

To his credit, economist Thomas Schelling did not let economic theory get in the way of learning about the real world. As he put it: "There is a tendency in our planning to confuse the unfamiliar with the improbable. The contingency we have not considered seriously looks strange; what looks strange is thought improbable; what is improbable need not be considered seriously."[40] To go back to Isaiah Berlin's metaphors, this is one reason why "hypothesis hedgehogs" who diligently pursue their well-developed "truths" are less successful than "fieldwork foxes" in the real world. The pragmatic foxes recognize the importance of being opportunistic by putting aside big plans that are unlikely to gain acceptance. They move on to shape and advocate for plans that stand a better chance in the hurly-burly political world. Hedgehogs ignore politics, with its unimaginable or unmanageable number of variables, and focus on substance. But they are more likely to find a real world that does not stand still for predictions or solutions that fail to account for the ever-changing and imperfect conditions. Silver, using Philip Tetlock's research, points out that "hedgehogs . . . [are] too stubborn to learn from their mistakes. Acknowledging the real-world uncertainties in their forecasts would require them to acknowledge the imperfections in their theories.[41] Those who are in the business of prediction are unable to foresee the future, so they use their talents to shape it. Tetlock also found that experts are prone to use the "hindsight effect" to imply that they knew more about what was going to happen than actually was the case.[42]

Fortunately, there are those who favor simulation techniques, instead of more static models. Simulation modeling is a process by which human interactions lead to new iterations. MIT'S Michael Schrage sees the value of the simulation process as generating "useful surprise"—a far cry from a static model.[43] Like behavioral economics, the simulation process incorporates human interactions, which are not easily contained or reliably projected in hold still models. More than likely, a useful simulation will challenge preexisting assumptions rather than confirm them.[44] Another dynamic process, which challenges hold still models and their assumptions, is the interdisciplinary research field of complex systems. "Complexity" is the study of emergent and self-organizing behaviors. Still a relatively young science, complexity has few settled assumptions that rule the field. However, it has influenced ways of thinking in terms of "nonlinearity, decentralized control, networks . . . and essential randomness."[45] Whenever I attend sessions at the Santa Fe Institute, which has done so much to house and advance the young science, I am intrigued, and often bewildered, by its interdisciplinary and collaborative ambitions. "Emergence," perhaps the institute's most provocative concept, challenges the linear thinking of disciplines and experts who feed primarily at one trough. Mitch Waldrop, who has a doctorate in elementary particle physics, offers a telling example of physicists at a Santa Fe Institute economics conference being empirically grounded as they challenged the assumptions made by the economists. The physicists asked: "'You guys really believe that?' The economists replied, 'If you don't make these assumptions, then you can't do *anything*.' But then the physicists countered, 'Yeah, but where does that get you—you're solving the wrong problem if that's not reality.'"[46]

The Coming of Credentialed Expertise

Beyond academe, credentialed specialization has firmly established the grounds of occupational security. The division of mental labor, like the division of manual labor, is more than just a matter of improving efficiency and production. It is also a means of social adjustment while limiting competition by dividing knowledge tasks into increasingly more specialized parts. Most credentialed specialists, at one time or another, have made a persuasive case that organizations needed their services. There is little dispute that the genuine needs of most organizations require specialized assistance; but organizational ignorance, like individual ignorance, leads to vulnerability to artful presentation or professional monopoly and can lead to being misled by the allure of esoteric knowledge. As far as most executives, managers, and administrators are concerned, the expert has had a tactical advantage. To follow the advice of a professional specialist is considered playing it safe.[47]

Ignorance is not a condition that most people willingly acknowledge, so America's culture of professionalism has led to a kind of well-meaning pretension on the part of ambitious professionals. Pretension in this case means letting others assume that you know more than you actually do. A specialist's pretension naturally arises when others are ignorant, including other specialists. Few professionals are likely to challenge each other's pretensions to spare themselves the disappointment of discovering or confirming that they share the same conceit. So credentialed specialists set up shop in a knowledge corner of their own, hoping to both impress and to serve others. Beyond academe, occupational pretension arises in any situation where the authority of knowledge is largely based on the credentialed positions reserved for it and not necessarily on the actual merit of an individual's performance. Some novice specialists may even be hired by an organization where they learn on the job what their credentials implied they already knew. This is especially true of those who have not acquired tacit knowledge from sufficient experience beyond the presentation of their credentials. When organizations establish credentialed positions, they create hundreds of niches that exclude perhaps potentially capable individuals who lack a turnkey credential. Randall Collins argued that "the great majority of jobs can be learned through practice by almost any literate person," including those who may lack professional credentials.[48]

Pretension can also arise among professionals who match their credentials to someone's personal needs. You don't have to agree with Ivan Illich's radical prescriptions in order to appreciate his then fresh 1970s criticism of professional mercenaries: "The income managers, lifestyle counselors, food faddist experts, sensitivity developers and others of this ilk clearly perceive the new possibilities for management, and move in to match commodities to the splintered needs and fractured self-confidence of the users."[49] At the same time, John McKnight wrote "if the servicer can effectively assert the right to define the appropriate question, he has the power to determine the need of his neighbor rather than meeting his neighbor's need."[50] Consider now the flourish of academic degrees that appear in solicitations online, through the mail, or on book jackets that offer the promise of usable knowledge by what the writer's credentials imply. Many Americans have become increasingly uncertain of their ability to rely on their own judgment and experience. The person who collects art may not delight in what he owns until assured by some expert that it is worth owning. The traveler may not really appreciate the ancient ruins until she has returned and been told that they were worth visiting. For literary critic Lionel Trilling, "The feeling grows among the educated classes that little can be experienced unless it is validated by some established intellectual discipline, with the result that experience loses much of its personal immediacy for us and becomes part of an accredited societal activity."[51] And the novelist Walker Percy observed that it "is not the fault of the expert. It is due altogether to the eager surrender of sovereignty by the layman so that he may take up the role not of the person but of the consumer."[52] How did this come about?

For much of the nineteenth century, problem solving was people-based. Land-seeking immigrants banded together into makeshift communities with self-governing practices established long before problem solving became knowledge-based. People-based problem solving arose from the dynamics of social relations and a homespun philosophy that boasted of the common sense of the common man. Members of these communities had a firm grasp of what they knew and, more important, what they needed to know. Their claim to knowledge was modest, but so were their communities' needs for it. What was necessary to know about most occupations was accessible to almost everyone. Tanning, spinning, repairing tools, the work of the miller, the blacksmith, the farmer—each found a niche in a simple division of labor, but they retained a general understanding of the nature and skills of each others' occupations.

In a simple community life, most Americans also had sufficient knowledge for the practice of self-rule. Given the remote and relatively limited role of state and federal governments, such self-rule emerged in conjunction with the establishment of practical "trades" in which "masters, journeymen, and apprentices" acquired certain forms of "economic independence."[53] Like the occupations of their neighbors, there was nothing esoteric about the knowledge that most Americans needed in order to organize and manage their local affairs. While the beginning of the American republic was essentially the organizing work of eighteenth-century land-owning gentlemen, democracy in the nineteenth century found its roots in less elite precincts. Historian Robert Wiebe concludes: "The revolutionary gentry arranged power; nineteenth century democrats diffused it."[54] Problems arose from local circumstance that most everyone could understand. Practical experience was more important than formal knowledge when citizens took part in making decisions that affected the life of their community. Thomas Jefferson's confidence in the potential of such folk was not misplaced—they had the necessary information and the common sense to govern their own affairs. No one was better suited to look after their local interests. For example, to this day in my rural neighborhood of northern New Mexico the community irrigation ditches ("acequias") endure as an example of self-rule. The gravity flow through such community ditches essentially comes from the snowmelt of surrounding mountains. A "mother ditch" is divided by gates that open and close, permitting each individual user to receive his water allotment when it comes to his assigned time to open his gate. The tradition of establishing and maintaining such man-made ditches has long been a necessary practice in a region that has to distribute the precious and limited resource of water to those needing it for their various agricultural purposes.

Nonetheless, in the late nineteenth century many of those living in tight little communities gradually lost their hold, as a national society was rapidly forming. Some of their neighbors, friends, and children moved away to stake a claim in growing cities, new universities, ambitious corporations, and public bureaucracies. Those staying behind could not claim to know the same things as those who were putting distance between their origins and the booming booster society that was becoming their new home. And so the need for education and formal training gained a place in a knowledge society taking hold. Attaining some kind of expertise created a portable credential of substantial value, and problem solving became more knowledge-based than people-based. Just as large organizations at the turn of the twentieth century lured many Americans away from their roots to seek new occupation status and income, newly formed public agencies arose in distant capitols seeking to keep pace with urban and industrial growth. The national society, which was forming out of a growing network of varied enterprises, required some amount of government regulation addressing new economic and social problems that were arising. It was a momentous adjustment for those who had been rooted in Jefferson's rural townships. Those who stayed put had to concede that public information, events, and decisions were no longer within the grasp of their local communities. The creation of the Federal Reserve Board, Federal Trade Commission, Interstate Commerce Commission, and passage of the Sherman Antitrust and Pure Food and Drug acts exemplified this move from local to national oversight.

No one raised this problem of adjustment with more insight than Walter Lippmann's *Public Opinion* in 1922: "The democratic tradition is . . . always trying to see a world where people are exclusively concerned with affairs of which the causes and effects all operate within a region they inhabit."[55] Lippmann, however, saw that such a tradition was fast expiring as the federal government displaced local government as the center of political life. And Lippmann came down firmly on the side of elected representatives having to rely heavily on experts to find solutions with only the tip of the hat to a Jeffersonian heritage. Lippmann argued that the progressive era, which took hold in the early twentieth century, required experts to help shape the policies and manage the problems that citizens could no longer control. Experts replacing citizens may be one reason why voting between 1896 and 1924 in national elections declined significantly. In 1896, 80 percent of voters turned out, by 1924 only 50 percent did. According to the historian, Robert Wiebe: "Early in the 19th century soaring turnouts among white men reinforced the impression of the People governing; early in the 20th century, falling turnouts reinforced the impression of people being governed."[56] Robert Westbrook offered a useful summary of the progressive era: "The democratic realists of the twenties focused their criticism of democracy on two of its essential beliefs: the belief in the capacity of all men for rational public action, and the belief in the practicality and desirability of maximizing the participation of all citizens in public life. Finding ordinary men and women irrational, and participatory democracy impossible and unwise under modern conditions, they argued that it was best to strictly limit government by the people and to redefine democracy as, by and large, government for the people by enlightened and responsible elites."[57]

Credentialed experts in government often treated "politics" as more the problem than the solution. When such experts focused on the substance of an issue without considering the politics, they pursued a necessary reductionism to eliminate the unmanageable number of variables that politics required. Nonetheless, specialists served with the expectation that they could provide answers that citizens and their elected representatives could not. Dewey took exception to such displacement, arguing that both expertise and citizens were needed. "The man who wears the shoe knows best that it pinches and where it pinches, even if the expert shoemaker is the best judge of how the trouble is to be remedied."[58] The credentialed expert, by virtue of his training, much preferred reason to action. If reason were central to problem solving, then the participation of citizens should follow, not precede, reason and whatever answers reason could provide. The citizen role in the progressive era was diminished in light of such professional expectations and the pretension that those with expertise had the answers. Furthermore, government service did not imply that those with credentials should ever surrender reason and yield to those they ostensibly served. On the contrary, for those with credentials—whether on a government payroll or advising citizens in their communities—assumed problem solving was more knowledge-based than people-based. Their specialized knowledge was meant to serve the interests and ignorance of those without such knowledge. For credentialed experts it made no sense that their "service" should kneel before an "ignorant" citizenry. James Morone, professor of political science, characterizes the progressive era as finding "a *best* way—precise, expert, scientific. The correct technique would yield the correct solution."[59]

The Professionalization of Government

The irony of the progressive era was the initial desire to take government back from political bosses, who were often corrupt, and give it back to "the people." In the process, however, professionals essentially took over parts of government in order to reform it—with the outcome of putting government beyond the reach of ordinary citizens.[60] Since the progressive era, the ambitious role of government has been sustained by a corps of policy experts and other professional specialists. Without "sunset" provisions in existing laws, government assumed a permanent place in social problem solving with experts close at hand. Such a corps could just as well have put a "No Help Wanted" sign in the government window informing citizens that those being served were not actually needed. By using credentials as trump, those in government with expertise unintentionally but seriously retarded the potential of a renewed civil society.

Consider the prominent role of policy analysts in government who seek to determine the "best" alternative for addressing a public problem. Most policy analysts use a microeconomics framework for the rational calculation of causes and results, as well as costs and benefits. However, when these analysts pursue a linear path of cause and effect to project likely outcomes of each alternative being considered, they rarely foresee a host of intervening variables that can produce unintended consequences. In addition, when policy analysts offer their best guesses of probable outcomes, they usually work only with the criteria and alternatives that *they* have selected. They also prefer quantifying the problems they frame and the alternatives they offer to decision makers, in whatever line of work public or private, who find such quantification an attractive form of measure. Just look at the rankings of colleges and universities, accounting profits, budget estimates, productivity measures, and resource depreciation. For example, there is the enduring prominence of cost-benefit analysis (CBA) that quantifies the negative and positive consequences of given alternatives. CBA is meant to determine whether projected benefits exceed projected costs of a particular policy option. CBA assumes that such consequences can be quantified in monetary terms, even for things not normally bought and sold in markets, such as clean air and water, peace and quiet, or even human life. Often, no one asks whether what is being valued is an appropriate subject for CBA. If some nonmarket good, such as human life, is being valued, should it be quantified to determine what policy option is chosen? There is the oft-cited case of a child trapped in an abandoned well where the rescue cost of x million exceeds the equivalent benefit of purchasing y mobile coronary units that can save z lives annually in the same community. CBA would be rightly concerned with the value of "statistical" lives, but the choice of decision makers to rescue the child would find the "identified" life at the bottom of the well more immediately compelling. Although quantification is unavoidable and no doubt a desirable shorthand, those using CBA are often not mindful that the "magic" of numbers can unnecessarily limit what others individually and collectively value.

Of course, we know that neither the progressive era nor any era thereafter has produced solutions to many of the problems that continually confront governments. The point is not that citizens could have done the job themselves. They certainly could not have. But the Lippmann expectations, shared by so many, turned out to be illusions: Too much faith had been placed in credentialed techniques. Significant contributions have been made by those with credentials, but knowledge-based problem solving has not won the day. The assumption that credentialed specialists could work *for* the public interest without working *with* the public proved to be false.[61] John Dewey, who was an ardent critic of the progressive era, and Alexis de Tocqueville long before him, saw that shutting citizens out of the process deforms their potential to be more knowledgeable and active.

Wide-ranging professionalized government and nongovernmental organizations have undermined the self-confidence of many Americans to look after problems within their reach or to collaborate with professionals, who often seem beyond their reach. Instead, they have settled for being the individual beneficiaries of professional knowledge who rarely band together as a social force to be reckoned with. The professional habit of condescending to layperson opinion and politics in general also gets in the way. And then there are the government precincts where many well-meaning professionalized public servants portray citizens as victims, or supplicants, or consumers—ignoring their potential to be partners in solving the problems that brought them to government's door in the first place. There is no end to the professional services rendered by public and quasi-public agencies—shelters for the homeless, shelters for battered women, child welfare departments, veterans administration services, vocational rehabilitation and training centers, community mental health programs, public assistance departments, and on and on. Harry Boyte, a social activist and theorist with keen insight and eloquence, describes the consequences: "As citizens became clients and consumers, the process hollowed out the civic muscle of mediating institutions, from local unions to civically grounded schools, business and voluntary associations."[62] The culture of professionalism has altered many people's conception of what their civic opportunities are and who is qualified to practice them. They have learned, or been persuaded, that the traditional habits for looking after others is not an adequate basis for becoming and staying engaged. It is not just a matter of letting someone else do it; it is standing aside in deference to professional credentials that seem superior to what citizens might offer. It is similar to the comment, "I don't have the answer, I'm not a doctor" or "I don't know enough, I'm not a lawyer" or "How can I know what stocks are worth buying, I'm not an investment banker." It even includes professionals themselves who have been conditioned to let a credential be the source and limit of their identity. Their socialization in academe of professional deference restrains them from exploring for themselves in fields of knowledge and practice apart from their own.

Many Americans are ambivalent about the professionalization of government. On the one hand, they have resolutely clung to the notion that "we, the people" know best, without being sure what they know or need to know in order to exercise responsible oversight of the activities of government. On the other hand, they have made insistent demands that government find efficient remedies for their problems but without too much cost or control. They have been led to believe that there are answers somewhere to be found by experts, who are trained to find answers, which will more than compensate for a citizen's marginal role. As a consequence, too many citizens only vote, let pollsters take their pulse, and then wait for someone to get the job done—regardless of whether those with credentials can ever find the answers and no matter whether citizens will readily accept such answers once they are found.

Unfortunately, "outsourcing" to credentialed specialists in government has been exacerbated by the media's frequent reliance on expert opinion with little critical distance on the part of news anchors and talk-show hosts. Their criticism, skepticism, or cynicism has been reserved for, and directed at, appointed and elected officials. Such public servants are considered fair game, but who's to know whether a credentialed specialist's recitation of facts and offering of opinion is reliable? It is easier to assume it is, given the media's dependence on expertise to provide credibility for whatever the newsworthy subject may be. The expert gets a pass if only to fill the hour with presumably better information and opinion than one expects from "those politicians, they're all the same." For "couch potato citizens," who are consumers of both media's wrinkled brow and the guru guests who add to media's legitimacy, such viewing is a vicarious experience that substitutes for the actual experience of getting up taking part in people-based problem solving. Michael Sandel at Harvard noted almost twenty years ago: "The global media and markets that shape our lives beckon us to a world beyond boundaries and belonging."[63] The practice of politics has not substantially changed, but many citizens have. They have digested media opinions and credentialed expertise with which to shape their judgments about the what and why of public life. Their ambivalence about getting involved may be a mixture of their own cynicism, competition for their time, and a sense of their inferiority when considering expert opinion constantly available to them through the media. "Thus, there are audiences, but no public."[64] I have written elsewhere: "Too many citizens seem content to let our public world become a spectator's arena for watching the politicians, pundits, and talking heads perform. Too many seem all too ready to fault government for doing too much or too little but rarely point the finger at themselves . . . Nonetheless, having become couch potato citizens, many sit back putting down government but at the same time putting up with it."[65]

Christopher Lasch once opined: "Meritocracy is a parody of democracy."[66] Meritocracy is evident when those leaving academe earn a place in the hierarchies of organizations or professional standing in the service of such organizations. Such success often excludes those who have lacked the resources or the will to achieve such status. They find themselves delegating to others in the culture of professionalism what should remain the prerogative of everyone, indeed the need for everyone, to restore the role of citizens in problem solving. Note the limited reach of problem solving with Alan Greenspan's comment that "everybody missed" the onset and severity of the 2008 "crash." Who was "everybody?" Greenspan cited "academe, the Federal Reserve and all regulators."[67] Obviously, a broad spectrum of players were sidelined by his comment. When citizens are just seen as victims or consumers, it privatizes them and they are no longer seen as participants. At best, they have become "special interests" needing professional advice, direction, and representation. The trump of credentials comes with a heavy price and is made all the more poignant by the fact that a good deal of knowledge, which is produced and applied by specialists, is really not beyond a citizen's experience and understanding. In *Usable Knowledge*, Charles Lindblom and David Cohen argued: "[M]uch of the 'new knowledge' produced [in the social sciences] is . . . ordinary knowledge. That is to say, it is produced by the same common techniques of speculation and casual verification that are practiced throughout the society by many different kinds of people, and is not by any significant margin more firmly verified."[68]

This is not the place to examine the relative merits of government policies that experts help to formulate or the government programs that they help to administer. Granted that elected representatives and bureaucrats should get all the help they can, given the enormous agenda that citizens presumably want them to pursue and administer. The point is not that experts are surplus baggage, but that too many of them have made citizens surplus baggage. Daniel Boorstin, the American historian, saw a terrible confusion in thinking that the maintenance of a democratic society primarily depends on finding answers to social and economic problems. "Our society has been most distinctively a way of reaching for rather than finding. American democracy properly speaking, has been a process and not a product, a quest and not a discovery. But a great danger which has been nourished by our success in technology has been the belief in solutions."[69] Government in America was meant primarily to be an arena for the contest of competing values, not just an agency for the rational solution of problems.

Increasingly, there is resistance on the part of some citizens to the continued use of professionalized government as a large, experimental laboratory to find "answers" for whatever ails the country. The contest between "credentialed" solutions and popular control has been joined of late, and it is likely to remain a major issue for the foreseeable future. Pretension, however, may still lead those with credentials to aggressively develop and offer solutions. They have something in common with the priests of ancient Greece. The ignorance of the people was the "foundation upon which the priest-power rested."[70] Thriving on ignorance, the advantage of such hierophants is not only their use of esoteric knowledge beyond popular understanding but also their claim that they have no personal interest or values that get in the way of finding the right solutions. They see politics, compromise, and consensus as the enemies of rational solutions, failing to acknowledge that there is nothing more rational than the assertion of individual and group self-interest or the necessity for compromise in the face of competing self-interests. A "truth" standard is hardly the standard by which Americans measure the acceptability of solutions when one person's truth may be another person's poison. The preoccupation of democratic government has been to address and adjust competing claims and conflicting objectives. Its feasible goal has been reconciliation. Of course, most practicing professionals do not make "truth" their standard. Lawyers, engineers, and many researchers and technicians do not pursue their own answers irrespective of a client's or sponsor's needs. I would be off-base to characterize experts in government, or in any organization that they try faithfully to serve, as truth seekers. I raise the problem of truth seeking in the context of the modern democratic process to show that whoever espouses its supremacy misunderstands that process. Frederick Hayek has argued: "The social process from which the growth of reason emerges must remain free from its control."[71] Certainly, there is no conspiracy afoot that will bring such a mentality to power. In fact, Steven Brint's study of the changing role of professionals in politics and public life led him to describe "a new 'expert' stratum with strong interests in marketable knowledge and weaker concerns about the relationship between community and authority."[72] Brint thinks of such experts as more "libertarian than liberal" and argues that the professional influence in government is exaggerated. Instead, what influence professionals have is with organizations "which are concentrated in the hands of leading interest groups and the leading politicians."[73] Nonetheless, such organizations are more than likely steered by professionally trained executives whose experience is very similar to their credentialed counterparts in government, both of whom may think credentialed expertise can deliver them from confusion or failure.

Notwithstanding Lippmann's cogent argument in the 1920s, citizens' parochial knowledge, which was defensible in that earlier era, is no less defensible now. The process of problem solving has too often excluded citizen input, which is nonlinear and dynamic. With linear decision making, professionals may diagram a process of clarifying objectives, surveying alternative means, identifying probable consequences of each alternative, and evaluating them in light of the objectives before making a choice. Such a linear process, however, is something like the proverbial drunk who searches for his lost key under the street lamp because the light is better there. "Wicked problems," around which there is moral and intellectual disagreement, are more amenable to the outcomes of people-based problem solving that can very well mitigate, if not resolve, wicked problems. Politics is far from being just a government practice, although too many mistakenly think so. Politics is embedded wherever citizens collaborate to deal with their wicked problems.

The Uses of Ignorance

Beyond academe, there are few organizations other than search engines, that try to promote public understanding of the knowledge produced by the division of mental labor. The media tries to simplify the grand enterprise of knowledge discovery and knowledge use, but such efforts are episodic and largely inadequate—promoting a confusion between information and knowledge. Electronic and print organizations midwife what they can sell, but any popularizations of expert knowledge challenge the powers of absorption, not reflection. The philosopher Jurgen Habermas commented on the paradoxical result that "the more the growth and change of society are determined by the most extreme rationality of processes of research, subject to the division of labor, the less rooted is this civilization, now rendered scientific, in the knowledge and conscience of its citizens."[74] The sociologist David Riesman went even further suggesting that the very division of mental labor has been in part responsible for a predicament of "meaning" for a public where the ambition for new knowledge and the way it has been organized makes it very difficult for anyone, including credentialed experts, to address such a predicament. Riesman recognized that such experts cannot responsibly pursue "a broad approach to the problems of society as a whole"—being "suspicious of the injudicious who make large plans" without the constraints of specialized knowledge. For Riesman, "utopia is a social order that has not been tried."[75]

Many findings of experts survive intact but their skeptical and critical minds are always in danger of affirming little other than their own powers. Riesman's predicament of "meaning" should not be considered an unruly guest at the high table of credentialed expertise. Concentrating on the remote nature of expertise ignores the fact that the expert also shares the layperson's desire for personal well-rounded meaning. Richard Hofstadter thinks it is a "fundamental fallacy" to separate the intellect "from all other human qualities with which it may be combined."[76] Experts are no less ignorant about most things than average citizens, and so it is possible that citizens *and* experts can find common ground where everyone has something to contribute and where everyone counts. The problem has been that for good reasons, and not so good reasons, most credentialed professionals continue to separate themselves from the lay public, choosing to define what they do with what knowledge they have without "reciprocal engagement with general public discourse."[77] This raises the problem of inadequate citizen feedback, which experts should have if they are to be more accurate in their knowledge development and more helpful with whatever professional judgment they can offer. It is such "task monopoly" that ill serves both experts and citizens.[78] There is less difference between serving members of the public and learning from them than many professionals might care to acknowledge.

The division of mental labor will no doubt continue, and credentialism will not soon disappear. Looking ahead, then, how can would-be professionals eventually prosper as experts without losing "the essential virtues of the amateur?"[79] The psychologist Abraham Maslow noted: "Science began originally as a determination to rely on one's own eyes instead of on the ancients or upon ecclesiastical authority or pure logic. That is, it was originally just a kind of looking for oneself rather than trusting anyone else's preconceived ideas."[80] Obviously, those without credentials cannot participate on the frontiers of science—that day is long past—but they can be introduced to the immense challenges to their ignorance that remain and share in the task of determining what it is they most want to know. The field of ecology has wisely seen the need for a critical science that explores questions that are vitally related to what amateurs need to know about organisms and their environments. The great mistake of any novice is to assume that the finished work or the accomplished act resembles the creative process that brought it into existence. How much of the fun and mystery is lost when students and laypersons devote themselves to acquiring the end product rather than appreciating how it was made. How very important it is for such "amateurs" to know that all that they admire in the rich possession of specialized knowledge was once as inchoate as their own vague intellectual ambitions. Listen to Emerson: "Meek young men grow up in libraries believing it is their duty to accept the views which Cicero, which Locke, which Bacon have given, forgetful that Cicero, Locke, and Bacon were only young men in libraries, when they wrote these books."[81]

Experts can therefore serve as catalysts rather than just authorities for the amateur. Experts can share their ignorance of what is not known in their respective fields, or what they do not know of other fields that bear upon the questions that both amateurs and experts consider worth pursuing. Experts can be indispensable guides for amateurs because such professionals are experienced in the art of learning, of using their ignorance. If the acknowledgement of ignorance is a healthy precondition for learning, it is what is often missing in today's credential seekers. Ignorance should not be seen as something to be covered over with the quick fix of getting a credential or the rituals of on-the-job-training. Ignorance is a permanent condition, not to be hidden by a credential, but to be used as the spur for long-lasting intellectual engagement. Therefore the professionalization of knowledge need not deter amateur curiosity and inquiry, nor should amateur ambitions be abandoned in the rush to master a piece of knowledge that provides an occupational identity. What a waste of talent and productive thinking when the amateur-turned-credentialed-specialist no longer feels qualified to use his ignorance outside his chosen field, and "[t]he remainder of life is treated superficially with the imperfect categories of thought derived from one profession."[82]

For those with credentials, who prefer to share their ignorance rather than hide it, the opportunity exists to use it, without hesitation or apology, with whatever gifts they have beyond their specialized knowledge. The "amateur" in experts, just like laypersons, can lead them to see that individual ignorance need not be a disability if it can be used as the healthy precondition for genuine learning. Lewis Thomas contends that we are "misled into thinking that bafflement is simply the result of not having learned all the facts . . . [when] we should be told that everyone else is baffled as well—from the professor in his endowed chair down to the platoons of post doctoral students in the laboratories at night."[83] The abundant production of knowledge, resulting from the division of mental labor, has obscured the obvious—that ignorance, not knowledge, has been the inspiration for such an enterprise. Intellectual ambitions have always been driven by what a person doesn't know or what he disputes that others think they know. For some professionals, their specialization may not yield sufficient and meaningful rewards, which is all the more reason that credentialed individuals should not neglect attending to their amateur questions. They have only to admit that a personal intellectual interest is what started them down the road in finding a specialty and gaining a foothold in topics that challenge them within their respective fields. Their amateur status was not relinquished when they became professionals. The amateur impulse to ask questions for personal reasons remains a valuable resource that they need not deny or ignore in themselves or others. Ignorance is undoubtedly a handicap but also an invitation to pursue what someone still has good reason to explore and learn.[84]

Chapter 5 takes up in detail how citizens and experts can deliberate together by sharing what each knows and doesn't know—a common ground of mutual ignorance that can become a new starting point where everybody counts: expertise and ignorance joined.

Phronesis for the Asking (I)

Marcus DeWitt's socialization in his graduate training led him to believe that government had become America's primary problem solver. DeWitt's credentials said as much with the beginnings of published work in academic journals focused on a variety of central planning initiatives by local governments. He had even written several op-ed pieces in the *Boot Valley Sentinel*, the local newspaper, arguing for more central planning by the town government if social problems such as obesity and the homeless were to be adequately addressed.

Soon to become an adjunct instructor in public administration, Dewitt had spent little time getting to know the town of Boot Valley lying below his university, which was perched high on a hill above the town. Most of his time was spent in his "cave," as he called it—a study carrel in the bowels of the university library. So one day, DeWitt decided to get out of his cave and off the hill. With no itinerary in mind, he descended into Boot Valley and wandered up and down. He eventually came across a long line outside a local bank.

"What's this all about," DeWitt asked a stooped man leaning on a shopping cart. "It looks like a run on the bank?"

"Oh, no, it's always this way when the ATM machine breaks down. They just don't have enough tellers."

"But why stand in line? It seems to me to be a suboptimal solution for such congestion."

The man shook his head. "Suboptimal—too big a word for me, but, my boy, a line is simply 'first come, first served.' It works for everyone . . . eventually."

Dewitt scratched his head. "Yes, of course, we all put up with lines, but isn't there a better way?"

The man shrugged. The line was moving. For him, that's all that seemed to matter. "A better way, like what?"

"Well, I'll have to give it some thought, but certainly the answer lies with the bank, not with you all out here."

As DeWitt moved on, he had to admit that "first come, first served" was often used to cope with social problems. He thought of the rights of seniority in employee relations, waiting lists for public housing, or for spaces in oversubscribed courses at his own university. In each instance, those waiting seemed to accept that "first come, first served" was an acceptable norm or, otherwise, it wouldn't be a norm. He began thinking that maybe he should look more carefully at other established "answers," which those in Boot Valley took for granted. DeWitt laughed at himself. "Maybe they were 'suboptimal,' but they were good enough when most everyone went along with them."

It wasn't long before DeWitt came upon a group of townspeople picking up litter on both sides of a road at the edge of town. DeWitt mumbled to himself, "Now that's something that government should surely be doing." Approaching the group, DeWitt asked: "Who deputized you all to do this work?"

Looking up from her bag full of trash, a woman immediately replied: "Deputize? No one deputized us! This was our idea—get rid of this ugly mess whenever we can." She paused. "Young man, the real challenge is rounding up enough friends and neighbors to get the job done. It's a never-ending search to find enough of them."

DeWitt politely countered: "But that's my point. Shouldn't this be the responsibility of Boot Valley's government?"

"Well," said another picker-upper close by, "who wants his property taxes raised to pay hired hands when we can get the job done ourselves?"

DeWitt assumed that taxes were always an issue in Boot Valley, as everywhere else. This ad hoc adopt-a-highway crew was taking responsibility for part of the road that apparently the town or county did very little about. DeWitt remembered reading about similar self-organization in nearby villages with residents looking after some of the local streams and beaches.

Just then, a "Town Harvest" truck passed by loaded with what DeWitt had been told was perishable food. The truck was probably on a delivery to that part of town where residents were regulars at food pantries and soup kitchens. Seeing that the truck had pulled over, DeWitt caught up to the driver, who was having a smoke, "Where do you guys get all this food?"

Taking a long drag on his cigarette, the driver replied, "Oh, I'm on my way to the Best Eastern Hotel, Ben's Hamburger Heaven, and Super Market Basket. You'd be surprised how much they would throw out the back if I didn't come 'round regularly. We even get some help from a community garden up the hill." DeWitt glanced up the hill and saw the spires of his campus. Why, had he never seen what the driver called a community garden? Taking a last puff, the driver added: "Hey, man, all we do is pool the resources around town and then get it to those most in need. Pretty slick, huh?"

DeWitt had to agree. Why would government need to have any role at all in such distribution? Now that he thought about it, pooling resources was the same thing that libraries, blood banks, and thrift shops did. And he knew that pooling manpower was what search parties and block-watches did, with no government in sight. As the Town Harvest truck pulled away, DeWitt thought to himself: "I'll have to get out more in the real world."

As he trudged back up the hill to the campus, DeWitt began to think that instead of believing government had the *answers* for those who lived in Boot Valley, he might better serve their interests by asking them questions:

- What unsolved social problems are within your range?
- What new social practices could you undertake along with enough others that might make a big difference?
- Have you heard about social initiatives that can't get off the ground, but where you and your neighbors joining in might make the difference?
- Do you know about existing social practices elsewhere that might also work in Boot Valley?
- As he passed by what he now realized was a community garden, DeWitt asked himself: "If I think that government can better solve the social problems of Boot Valley, what are the likely costs and how will they be paid for? And if a particular social problem requires a new law or local ordinance, is there likely to be general compliance? Will it ever be scrapped once it's in place?

The more DeWitt constructed questions in his mind, the more he realized that whatever "answers" he might provide, or government for that matter, would be beside the point—Boot Valley citizens were needed to make any answers really work. He remembered the remark of the woman on the cleanup crew about finding "enough others." DeWitt thought to himself, "If everyone else is going to pick up trash, why do they need me? But if my cooperation is important in enlisting or maintaining others' cooperation, then I become important—not just an accessory. Maybe the conditional nature of most people's cooperation was a strength, not a weakness."

DeWitt was beginning to realize he had a lot of work ahead of him—his credentials were nice but far from enough. Walking the streets of Boot Valley, both his knowledge *and* his ignorance had been joined. He smiled. "So this is what Aristotle had in mind about practical wisdom." DeWitt had found *phronesis*, not up on campus, but down in Boot Valley just for the asking.

CHAPTER 3

Self-Serving Professionals

The legacy of serving others is part of the culture of professionalism, but today the culture is some distance from traditional expectations. Consider the stories we have already heard about "professionals" in the finance industry—bankers, credit rating agencies, and advisers of all kinds—who, like apprentices of an absent sorcerer, were caught up in the enterprise of fevered and often indiscriminate production of collateralized debt obligations that led to the Great Recession. When clients, patients, or others in need of advice and support do not fully understand what professionals do, they have to trust that a professional's knowledge is valuable and necessary and, more important, that the professional is putting their interests first. The primacy of "service" explains why professions have been allowed a much greater degree of self-regulation than other guilds in the marketplace. The influence of America's religious history shaped the very concept of service leading on to secular forms of "social trusteeship" as professionals assumed an almost paternal role in serving others' interests. With the antecedents of America's religious institutions and the "social trustee" model that developed among nineteenth-century professionals, the traditional norms of professionalism have been to "adhere to a service ideal [and] devotion to the client's interest more than personal or commercial profit . . . when the two are in conflict." According to Harold Wilensky, "the service ideal is the pivot around which the moral claim to professional status revolves."[1]

For better or worse, the culture of professionalism rests, in part, on a kind of unstated pretension that professionals know far more than they actually do or clients or patients think they do. To some extent such pretension is unavoidable because layperson reliance on professionals is all the more secure if they believe professionals have the requisite knowledge to help them—whether they do or not. However, the mystery of what professionals know, or what laypersons think professionals know, can be abused by self-serving professionals. In this chapter I use "industry" rather than "profession" to discuss the law, medical, and finance industries, to underscore the increasing fixation on profit of self-serving professionals. Profit and service are not necessarily antithetical, but the balance between them has been altered. Some lawyers, doctors, and financial advisers pursue what might be called the production and sale of their services, making their chosen endeavor more a business than a profession. Of course, any professional might counter by saying: "Yes, my job is, in fact, to serve my own interest but professionally cultivated, so that the fruit of my self-directed labor benefits the interests of others—others who, by virtue of their lack of expertise, could not possibly have as well-trained an eye for what is in their interest." Such a rationalization is plausible but far from convincing when a professional's self-interest *conflicts* with rather than complements the interests of those he presumably serves. Enlightened self-interest is when others gain something, too. I have written elsewhere that professionalism can be seen as "an organizing impulse, an accommodating rationale for enlightened self-interest that nonetheless is meant to serve larger public interests."[2] Professor Albert Dzur of Bowling Green University told me in an interview: "Since the 1960s, public opinion regarding many professions has been increasingly skeptical as the social trustee image of doctors, lawyers, academics, and others has been tarnished by what appears to be a rise in self-seeking behavior on the part of practitioners."[3] This is partly due to the increasing number of professionals and consequently the increasing competition among them. And that calls for a look at the legal industry.

The Law Industry

As someone trained in the law, who practiced on Wall Street, and provided legal counsel in federal and state precincts as a government official, I know such experience was invaluable. But the subsequent road that I traveled did not prepare me for the shock of what law schools and law firms have done, or not done, just in this new century. As a consequence, the legal profession has become the target for some very pointed criticism. Of course, lawyers have always been targets, which naturally arises from their strategic position of initiating, as well as resolving, for better or worse, a wide range of contested issues, both private and public. The criticism of late, however, has focused on the excessive self-serving behavior of law deans, law faculty, and law partners in private practice. Such criticism portrays them less as custodians of a profession and more as opportunists in organizations where bottom-line profit and loss comes before serving interests other than their own. Consequently, I think the "legal industry" is a suitable description for what has been going on. Stephen Harper, a former practitioner and a critical observer of the current legal scene, does not mince words: "From law schools to the pinnacle of the profession at America's most prestigious law firms, unrestrained self-interest—let's call it greed—has taken key legal institutions to an unfortunate place."[4] At a time when technology has greatly reduced the time factor in billable hours, it can be argued that such firms have increased their fees to compensate, and shortchanged their own law associates whose hours are billed out at rates that far exceed what they are paid by their firms. With such mark-ups, firms ill serve their clients as well as their own associates. Harper points out that some firms will bill out associate time at $400 per hour making a tidy profit for themselves.[5] "With the assistance of management consultants who are not lawyers, most leaders of large firms have pushed their firms away from their professed ethos and toward the outer limits of their potential as profit-generating enterprises."[6]

The original focus of graduate-school educated lawyers, as opposed to the apprentice model prevailing during much of the nineteenth century, was to raise the bar for those who sought admission to practice. The new home for the legal profession in academe also had the effect of excluding those who were thought to be socially inferior in an Anglo-Saxon dominated profession.[7] There was just a half-century or more of such class fixation, however, and in the latter half of the twentieth century, both elite law schools and law firms made a substantial effort to be inclusive rather than exclusive for Waspish aspirants. Acquiring wealth through law practice came to take the place of achieving social status as an end of itself. Many big city law firms began to pay more attention to profit making. Mark Harris, who left a big Wall Street firm to found Axiom Law, contends that "the interests of law firms went from serving clients to serving themselves." Axiom Law has 900 lawyers, no partners, and charges less than the elite law firms for routine legal work that doesn't require high fees.[8]

When acquiring wealth becomes a primary motivation in any professional organization, that organization can become unstable if those in it look for even more wealth in some other competing organization that is on the make or on the rise. Lateral transfers from one law firm to another, which were once thought of as little more than professional treason, are now quite common—it's every man for himself. It should be noted that women have not markedly increased their numbers in recent years as a percentage of equity partners in big city law firms. Harper argues that another consequence of the "wealth" standard replacing social status is the increasing "income inequality" among lawyers in big city firms. "The singular focus on compensation . . . rewards bad behavior—hoarding clients, demanding more billable hours . . . In the process, it often destabilizes the law firms themselves."[9] A former law partner of mine and celebrated author, Louis Auchincloss has always been a perceptive observer of his social class and also of his profession. Auchincloss told the not-so-fictional story of Robert Service, a corporate lawyer, in *Diary of a Yuppie*. In discussing the book, William Sullivan singles out Service, whose last name was not a careless choice by Auchincloss, as an example of a generation "having to validate their self-worth through comparative ranking along an infinite scale of wealth and power." Sullivan argues that Auchincloss wanted to chronicle how "the old gentry ethic of the free professions" had "been ousted by the purely strategic orientation of finance" and the "blatantly mercenary professionalism" that "evolved as a response to an increasingly dangerous and bellicose economic scene."[10]

Part of the problem for the legal industry is that the U.S. has too many lawyers, more than any country in the world relative to its population, which exacerbates the competitive stress within the profession. "When a profession such as the law grows four times as fast as the population, it is not surprising that a great many lawyers in their struggle to make a living treat law as a trade solely for profit."[11] Such competition has greatly affected the ongoing conflict that any professional feels when trying to reconcile his self-interest with the interest of a client. Increasing competition in the profession, however, does not mean that legal services have been made available to a greater range of potential clients. The profession has left that to lawyers not caught up in wealth seeking who choose instead to represent clients who cannot afford to pay what are often very expensive legal fees. It is paradoxical that so many law school graduates currently find themselves without work as lawyers, and yet so many Americans find that they can't afford the legal services that they need. There are some healthy signs, however, that such a contradiction may be addressed more actively than in the past. For example, there is a nonprofit law firm that Arizona State University has established and a new program, Lawyers for America, initiated by the University of California Hastings College of the Law to put their students and graduates into real-world organizations that offer legal services to those who cannot afford them.

The unrelenting competition among law schools for enrollments in a stagnant economy has also victimized their graduates who increasingly discover, usually too late, that the amounts they have borrowed and paid to secure a credential over three years is no longer a guarantee of gainful employment. Brian Tamanaha, a professor of law at Washington University in St. Louis, has described in detail why law schools' "hunger for revenue and chase for prestige" ill serves a generation of would-be lawyers who cannot find good legal jobs after graduation and have to start paying off the staggering amount of debt that their law school education caused them to take on. Harvard Law graduates had an *average* debt of $115,000 in 2010. The annual tuition at Yale Law School in 1987 was $12,450. In 2010 it had more than quadrupled to $50,750. For law school students graduating in 2010 their aggregate debt was more than $3.6 billion.[12] Adding insult to injury: "About a third of graduates in the past decade have not secured jobs as lawyers within nine months after graduation."[13] In 2009 only 71 percent of law school graduates "secured any job requiring bar passage." In 2010 only 68 percent did, and in 2011 it was 55 percent.[14] There are exceptions, of course, with starting pay for some novice lawyers reaching $160,000 in big city firms, plus a year-end bonus. Such exceptions, however, have not changed the overall trend when in 2004 there were 100,000 law school applicants, but the estimate for 2012–2013 was only 54,000.[15]

Why are law schools so expensive? A good deal of the tuition revenue is consumed by faculty "scholars," who publish law review articles mainly for the benefit of their faculty peers and seek to command ever more well-paying academic salaries. What they are paid in no way rivals what they might make in private practice, but it is quite generous considering how few hours they teach. Teaching loads have declined to accommodate those preoccupied with their "scholarship." They spend up "to a third less time in the classroom than earlier generations."[16] The majority of their work time is often set aside for writing dense, specialized pieces, many of which have little to do with the practice of law. Apparently, legal experience outside of academe is not considered to have much value for what one produces in law review articles. A 2010 study found that since 2000, "nearly half" of the faculty hires at top-tier law schools "had never practiced law for a single day."[17] Harper quotes an adjunct professor who said "the academy wants people who are not sullied by the practice of law. A lot of people who are good at big ideas, the people who teach at law school, think it is beneath them."[18] It is not surprising then that a 2005 study found that 40 percent of the law review articles in the Lexus-Nexis database had never been cited in cases or even in other law review articles.[19] In 2011, Supreme Court Chief Justice John Roberts concluded: "What the academy is doing . . . is largely of no use or interest to people who actually practice law."[20]

The collective ambition of many law school faculties seems to be not so much training lawyers as it is maintaining a respectable place for themselves among their peers in academe. It is another example of how being separated from the real world encourages work in academe that is "too self-referential."[21] It is little wonder that the cost of a legal education has climbed so much with some elite law professors commanding salaries exceeding $300,000 and reduced teaching loads necessarily requiring more faculty hires to compensate. As a consequence, there is increasing evidence that many law schools and the universities that support them may be flirting with fiscal bankruptcy. And for this lawyer-trained observer, such shortsightedness may also be a form of moral bankruptcy when professors use their professional standing primarily to find a comfortable refuge in academe and when administrators turn their law schools into desperate profit centers of increasing enrollments even as many of their graduates cannot find employment in their chosen field.[22]

The Medical Industry

Characterizing medical practice as an industry is obviously not a perspective that many doctors, nurses, and others would share. Nonetheless, like some lawyers, some practicing doctors have used their professional standing to reap profits and make the bottom line more important than serving the interests of their patients. Because so much of their patients' health costs are paid for by health insurance, it is perhaps easier for such doctors to look after themselves first without patient resistance. Those insured may pay little attention to the cost of such services and want no cost spared when addressing whatever their doctor or they think afflicts them. In a recent study, "patients for the most part did not want cost to play any role in decision making."[23]

It is common knowledge that some doctors overtest their patients. It is often prompted by their fear of malpractice litigation, but it is also the consequence of some doctors owning the test equipment to be used and seeking to recover their investment and a profit from its frequent use. Some doctors may seem too ready to prescribe X-rays, CT scans, or MRI tests for lower back pain. According to *Consumer Reports*, "research suggests that those who invest in imagery equipment order more CT scans and MRI tests than doctors who haven't made the investment."[24] Investigators from the Government Accountability Office reported: "Doctors who have a financial interest in radiation treatment centers are much more likely to prescribe such treatments for patients with prostate cancer."[25] Overtesting for profit is one cause of spiraling health-care costs. By some estimates it is part of what constitutes one-third of medical spending in the United States, which also includes "unnecessary hospitalization, unproven treatments [and] ineffective new drugs and medical devices."[26]

Such unnecessary testing may increase when the Baby Boomer generation who, like it not, have to encounter the medical industry in their twilight years, and the industry like a python tries to swallow that pig. One observer, Peter Bach, MD, thinks that money is not at the heart of overtesting; it is a culture problem of "the doctor knows best." But as Dr. Bach points out, "We are terrific at inventing new tests that can be performed on people. But we have been less good at figuring out which people should have them."[27] A pharmacist, however, pointed out to me that doctors have to deal with "the backlog in many hospitals and labs." It is "prudent for a clinician to take care of as many needs as possible in his or her office for reasons of earlier detection and verification of treatment path, and this possibly *decreases* overall cost due to missed or late detected issues."[28] Whether or not the excessive caution of some medical practitioners makes sense, it is part of a long story of how doctors are educated and how the hierarchy of the profession insulates too many doctors from the questions of subordinates and patients who might challenge their medical opinions if only the culture was less entrenched. The traditional hierarchical structure of the medical profession has been for doctors to be on top and everyone else, including patients, beneath them.

Doctors, however, are not the only critical players in the medical industry. It also includes those who manufacture and sell testing equipment, and the ever-present pharmaceutical companies, which, for better or worse, go to great lengths and expense to convince doctors that their patients need their merchandise. And there are some members of the medical profession who have become more than just customers. They have become profit-seeking partners in moving the merchandise. Whether it is overtesting or overtreatment with drugs, which may do little good and sometimes can do great harm, some doctors are taking advantage of their professional standing at the expense, both human and fiscal, of the American public. It may start when pharmaceutical salesmen provide free samples to doctors, who in turn provide free samples to their patients, who will eventually start paying for them. There is nothing necessarily wrong with such generosity on the part of the pharmaceutical companies or doctors except that a doctor's preference for a particular drug may be corrupted by being paid an honorarium on the side for his ostensible medical judgment with respect to the drugs being offered in his office. For example, it was reported that one "infectious disease specialist" was paid $340,754 by drug companies in 2011.[29] Most doctors, however, are conscientiously looking for medical products that really work, and new tests and treatments are a part of that search. No doubt, there will be some "waste" in retrospect, but there is an important difference between marketing uncertain products and the fact that some doctors reap financial gain regardless of the efficacy of a product.

No doubt medical practice offers several other profit-making, and sometimes corrupt, possibilities. One is the otherwise valuable practice of making greater use of electronic record-keeping, which in the right hands can be a more efficient delivery of medical services. In the wrong hands, doctors can enter data of exams that never took place. The potential for fraud has become considerable.[30] Another corrupt practice is when "business-minded doctors . . . reroute profitable patients from general multi-specialty hospitals to specialty hospitals in which the doctors hold an interest." William Hanson, MD, says that "the doctor-owner thus gets the professional fees for his own work as well as a second bite of the apple from the specialty hospital's profits. This is Darwinism at work in medicine—the strong wresting resources from the weak."[31] And some doctors and dentists, whose services are not adequately covered by various forms of insurance, offer the financing plans of outside companies to patients with the health-care provider being paid up front. For many patients, especially the elderly, the terms of such financing can be misunderstood or elusive. "Attorneys general in . . . several states have filed lawsuits claiming that . . . professionals have misled patients about the financial terms . . . employed high pressure sales tactics, overcharged for treatments and billed for unauthorized work."[32] However, blaming some doctors for their avarice will hardly settle things. Jane Brody of the *New York Times*, an outspoken observer of the health scene, sees the larger picture of a health-care system sparing no expense to detect ill health but promising "to bankrupt us without necessarily improving our health."[33] With the fee-for-service system still in place, "hospitals and doctors are reimbursed for performing lots of procedures and tests regardless of whether they are necessary to make their patients get better. Providers who excel and achieve better outcomes with fewer visits, procedures and complications are penalized by being paid less."[34]

Fortunately, there are many professionals in the medical industry who are strategic, not just the doctors—think of pharmacists, nurse practitioners, physician assistants, those in "retail" clinics, home health-care aides—all of whom can deliver primary care that is often the equal of the doctors at the top of the heap. Some doctors welcome such alternatives, others may not, but the medical profession is likely to become less hierarchical as such primary care providers continue to prove their worth. Perhaps it is inevitable since there is an ongoing shortage of primary care physicians, a shortage made more evident with health coverage supposedly being extended in 2014 to an additional thirty million Americans. "Supposedly" is a necessary qualification given the enormous problems that confront the Affordable Care Act. One crude fact, however, helps to explain the shortage of primary care doctors who earned on average about $200,000 in 2010 while many medical specialists made twice that amount.[35] H. Gilbert Welch, a professor of medicine at the Dartmouth Institute for Health Policy and Clinical Practice, sees the state of the medical industry as "a problem of perverse incentives; good people working in a bad system . . . Ultimately, society needs individuals to be guided by ethical standards. And in medical care, those standards are getting pretty darn low."[36]

Under the Affordable Health Act of 2010 those enrolled in Medicare are entitled to an "annual wellness visit" with a doctor who doesn't have to find something wrong in order to get paid. The concept of affordable

health care assumes that everyone should be able to get professional attention for whatever ails each person, without having to pay an arm and a leg
to get it. It's a nice idea but misses the point that this country will not be
able to meet the costs of such professional attention unless Americans do
more on their own to look after themselves and to look after those family
members, friends, coworkers, and neighbors in need of more attention
and care. To think that the medical industry will do it for them is wishful thinking. Learning to eat better, to exercise regularly (on any given
day, nearly 40 percent of Americans don't exercise at all), and looking
out for others are vital forms of "health care," too. Nearly 40 percent of
the annual mortality rate in the United States has been traced to poor
diet, physical inactivity, smoking, and abuse of alcohol.[37] Think of the
people of every age who are obese and at risk for diabetes and heart disease. Of the approximate $2.5 trillion that the federal government spends
on health care annually, almost $150 billion goes to paying for obesity-
related conditions. Of course, the medical industry is there to help, but
other industries—food and beverage in particular—stand to profit from
the status quo. Listen to the popular author about food Michael Pollan:
"There's a lot of money to be made selling fast food and then treating
the diseases that fast food causes. One of the leading products of the
American food industry has become patients for the American health care
industry."[38] And the health costs of those who are obese are 72 percent
greater than those for people of normal weight.[39]

What gets left out so often when examining America's medical industry is that most doctors are knee-deep in disease care, not health care.
For good reasons, and not so good reasons, such an industry promotes
and prolongs patient dependence without much attention to nurturing
patient capacities to take better care of themselves. That is why those
professionals who labor in public health are likely to become even more
essential intermediaries when their services include vaccinations, motor
vehicle safety, safer workplaces, control of infectious diseases, safer and
healthier foods, family planning, and many other critical initiatives.[40]
Furthermore, affordable care out of necessity will likely unsettle the traditional hierarchy that now relies mainly on doctors to have the know-how
and authority to truly serve their patients' needs. Fortunately, such reliance
is already being modified by primary care doctors who are using a team
approach with support staff motivating and encouraging patients to do
more for themselves. Nurturing patient capacities rather than prolonging

their dependence is still at the margins of most medical practices, but it is likely to become more prominent considering the shortage of primary care doctors available to the aging Boomer generation for the foreseeable future. There are only 7,000 geriatric physicians for the 10,000 Boomers who will turn 65 *every day* for the next fifteen or so years, and it is estimated that the shortage of primary care doctors may amount to 150,000 by 2025.[41]

The Finance Industry

The finance industry, unlike law and medicine, is a mix of credentialed professionals and profiteers who pass themselves off as professionals. In looking back at the financial swoon of 2007–2009, it is difficult to distinguish between the two. Before the financial swoon there was a shortage of trustworthy, expert judgment serving the investing public. Honest advice is generally in shorter supply than the investing public may realize, and when the financial swoon overwhelmed almost everyone, this fact was made abundantly clear. Who were the professionals and who were the profiteers who earned fees for managing others people's money? They both had clients and customers and claimed that they had the expertise to serve their interests. (Does "their interests" seem ambiguous here? I intend it as such, because whose interests came first is far from clear.)

The financial swoon arose, in part, when many collateralized debt obligations (CDOs), which are pools of mortgage payments, were packaged and sold proving to be little more than junk. Nonetheless, it was a lucrative play for both professionals and profiteers. Bankers created a credit laundering service for those who could ill afford the borrowing costs associated with homeownership. Such bankers routinely approved shaky loans in the form of home mortgages for many prospective home-buyers with little income and few or no assets, and then the same bankers routinely sold the so-called subprime mortgages to Wall Street playmakers. Best-selling author Michael Lewis aptly summarized that banks could keep on making loans to people who couldn't repay them, as long as the banks didn't keep the loans on their books. The point was to "sell them off to the fixed-income departments of big Wall Street investment banks, which [would] in turn package them into bonds and sell them to investors."[42] It was a game that professionals played assuming that if someone had to lose, it wouldn't be them. Later, there was a lot of finger pointing at borrowers, some of whom misrepresented their financial specifics, bankers who just didn't care as long as they could sell such risky products and get it off their books, and at the Wall Street playmakers who sold mortgage-backed securities to unsuspecting investors worldwide. Many investors didn't understand the risks they had assumed. They had trusted the recommendations of their professional advisers.

Included in this "securitization" mix were the credit rating agencies, such as Moody's and Standard & Poor, whose role is ostensibly to offer objective assessments of the creditworthiness of a variety of financial instruments issued and sold to the investing public. Such agencies stood to one side but reaped substantial profits when giving CDOs and other mortgage-backed securities a triple-A rating—AAA meaning they were as secure as U.S. government bonds. Wall Street profiteers paid lucrative fees to the credit raters for these generous ratings. Standard & Poor claimed that there was only a "0.12 probability—about 1 chance in 850—that [a CDO] would fail to pay out over the next five years."[43] Nate Silver concludes that "the boom in subprime lending was financed by investors who were told they had supersafe securities. The bubble would not have happened without S & P and its peers."[44] Ultimately, the International Monetary Fund put losses of U.S.-originated subprime-related assets at a trillion dollars.[45] And according to Andrew Sorkin of *The New York Times*, the financial industry has not changed much since the swoon. "Of 250 industry insiders who responded to questions—traders, portfolio managers, investment bankers, hedge fund professionals, financial analysts, investment advisers, among others—twenty-three percent said that 'they had observed or had firsthand knowledge of wrongdoing in the workplace' . . . If the report is accurate, the insidious culture of greed is back—or maybe it never left."[46]

Blind Spots in Academe

What accounts for the decade-long period of malfeasance or negligence by those considered to be professionals in the financial industry? Some would think that it is just a few bad apples in the barrel. Others would think it is the ever-increasing desire to get rich and stay rich above all else. Still others fault independent accountants, boards of directors, and government agencies for failures of "oversight." And fingers also point at poorly managed banks, careless credit-rating agencies, and indifferent regulators. What we lost was trust in those who we thought were supposedly looking after our interests and not just their own. It was a moral failure, not just a market failure. Obviously, there are many to share the blame. One substantial player, however, goes unscathed: academe, which seems increasingly preoccupied with preparing students to make a living, with little consideration of how to live. Andrew Ross Sorkin reported on a "controversial study called 'Economics Education and Greed' . . . published in 2011 by professors at Harvard and Northwestern." The study claims "that economics education is consistently associated with positive attitudes towards greed . . . [given] . . . the uncontested dominance of self-interest maximization as the primary (if not sole) logic of exchange."[47]

Another observer, Dr. Jonathan Macey of Yale Law School, has added a new and troubling perspective about why the financial debacle happened as it did. Macey sees "reputational capital" as no longer valued by professionals on Wall Street. Reputation was once an important asset, acquired and preserved, but Macey argues that increased federal regulation, the Securities and Exchange Commission (SEC) in particular, has superseded and eliminated reliance on "reputational capital." And, according to Macey's argument, "reputational intermediaries," like accounting firms, law firms, and credit-rating agencies, are also off the hook. What makes Macey's argument troubling is that it seems driven by his reliance on cost-benefit analysis devoid of any moral equilibrium. Applying a cost-benefit approach to theft, Macey argues: "The theory of reputation posits that firms will not invest in developing reputations for honesty and trustworthiness unless the benefits from making such investments are greater than the costs."[48] Macey goes so far as to say: "Firms with solid reputations will refrain from cheating as long as profits garnered from such cheating are lower than the losses from whatever reputational damage the fraud is likely to produce."[49]

This argument reflects a kind of amoral neutrality. Here is a professor of law, with a doctorate in economics and affiliated with Yale's School of Management, who uses cost-benefit analysis and assumes that "reputation," which heretofore has been considered honest service, is no longer valued because federal regulation has become the primary monitor of professional conduct.[50] Is it any wonder that with such cold-blooded cost-benefit assumptions that many would-be professionals in graduate classrooms may become more cynical and opportunistic about the world they will enter? There have always been frauds and outliers in any realm of professional practice, but it is troubling when graduate school instruction theorizes that cost-benefit analysis makes fraud a circumstantial phenomenon. Macey does not deny the possibility of alternatives to reputation—such as religious and ethnic affiliations, social networks, and self-help—but his theorizing reinforces the very market world he would find unacceptable. As I argued in Chapter 2, assumptions in academe are critical and telling, and here a well-meaning professor of law has all but abandoned the possibility that would-be professionals, as moral individuals, can find alternatives of their own that are not driven by the prevailing ethos of current organizations. No doubt, most would-be professionals are likely to follow the crowd in a culture of professionalism, but when the theories and analytic practices of those who teach in academe offer little or no alternative, then the programs at these institutions resemble indoctrination more than education.

Consider the example of "front-running," which is when a financial adviser has his firm buy or sell securities in advance of orders already placed by his clients. Do professors such as Macey give equal time to educating their would-be professionals about what constitutes a breach of trust, or do they remain morally neutral and offer descriptive, rather than prescriptive, observations of a financial industry practice and why investors have made greater use of index funds?[51] In his treatise, Macey argues for less SEC regulation, which he thinks would restore "reputation" as the necessary asset in doing a profitable business with strangers. But he ignores entirely the potential role of education to do more with the moral imagination in the precincts where economic theory still holds sway. If, according to Macey, reputation is "out-of-order," then professional service, as traditionally understood, is in serious jeopardy.

Consider another blind spot in academe. Professional service in academe—which is part of the traditional triangulation of scholarship, teaching, and service—can often mean little more than adequate "internal service," the shared governance of committee work and disciplinary service that amounts to "reading proposals and papers for conference presentation" and "editing journals and newsletters."[52] Consider the experience of a humanities scholar who told me: "My colleagues kept getting annoyed with my insistence that we focus attention on teaching and the public impacts (actual and potential) of candidates' scholarship. They considered these criteria 'left overs' and 'fallbacks' and signs of failure, in effect, for those who could not make the grade. . . . The notion of the professional as status keeper (achievement criteria, reputation, separation from the pack) effortlessly trumps an 'ethic' of the professional life of generative commitment and moral purpose—a life of care. So the distinction I am trying to make is a very basic and simple one between values and guild expertise."[53]

It's fair to say that academe has become corrupted in its own way with too many institutions running after too few potential students in what remains the most decentralized higher education system in the world. Lately, American colleges and universities have used the language of "markets" and "consumers" to describe their student prospects with the simple model of "economic man," a self-interested, maximizing creature coming to the fore. Such language can infect the minds of would-be professionals who are more eager to find convenient answers than to ask hard questions about what should motivate them in the real world. When a financial adviser blithely or willfully ignores the interests of those he ostensibly serves, it may be that he has never been educated to consider interests other than his own. Many professional schools have apparently failed to educate, not just train, a generation of wannabe investment bankers, hedge fund managers, and corporate executives. They have carelessly trained their graduates "to go forth and get yours" without educating them to the moral ties that necessarily exist between lenders and borrowers or between issuers and investors. Somewhere along the way "success" has become equated mainly with big bonuses and bank accounts.

Training describes learning how to perform specific tasks. *Education* promotes, among many other things, values and sensibilities that have sustained Americans as a people that go way beyond the simple model of "economic man." Trained, but not well educated, too many would-be professionals have taken for granted that the pursuit of self-interest is all that is required to make markets function effectively, even though the causes of the financial swoon belie such shallow confidence. Why has academe let them down? Like so many of their universities' graduates, administrators have become more or less fixated on short-term, bottom-line outcomes for their universities and the return-on-investment expectations of students and parents. They have treated their would-be professionals as "customers" who seek the credentials they think they need for the good life, but their faculty colleagues have too often neglected to provide examples of what a "good life," in the classical sense, is. Here and there in the curricula moral questions are entertained but certainly not pursued with the same attention as developing critical analytic and quantitative capacities. Many graduates soon find themselves managing other people's money but lacking the moral compass that their clients expect and deserve.

I recall one of my graduate faculty colleagues saying with exasperation, "Tell me, David, which discipline, which department should have the expertise to address what you and I would call 'moral concerns?'" My reply was, "All of them." At whatever level, the distancing from moral concerns in favor of bloodless academic neutrality does not well serve students who have to sort out not just what to do with their credentials but who they are or what they want to become. Trustees, administrators, faculty, and students must find ways to pursue new or revised initiatives that address the moral vacuity in institutional research, teaching, and even "service learning," as captured in one student's comment that he hoped there would still be soup kitchens when his children reached college age. Unfortunately, both administrative and academic leaders increasingly neglect or shortchange their humanities scholars and curricula, which are not moneymakers but are still indispensable for educating the whole person. Michael Oakeshott once wisely noted: "A university is not a machine for achieving a particular purpose or producing a particular result; it is a manner of human activity."[54] And much of that activity is a never-ending conversation about human ends, not just human means. Whatever the credentialed ambitions of its students, a university can do no better than to engage them in that conversation.

More "ethics" courses are not enough as a curricular gesture in universities that pursue business as usual in the mercenary, professional cultures many have settled for. "Professional ethics," a staple of self-regulation, is sometimes cited as the enduring and authoritative basis for judging professional conduct.[55] Professional ethics, however, is rarely cited as a means of correcting self-interested professional conduct. When I inquired about the subject, one academic-emeritus simply replied: "To tell the truth, in 33 years I can't think of one time when the phrase 'professional ethics' passed the lips of a colleague, or chair, or dean. I should say, passed from lip service into action."[56] Another senior scholar thought that "both moral philosophy and, more narrowly, professional ethics ought to be integrated into graduate programs . . . It remains irresponsible *not* to connect education that will inform consequential action with moral reflection, ethical reasoning, and practices of judgment."[57] I was interested to learn that a scholar engaged in an interdisciplinary field of art and philosophy has been working with a group of colleagues on what they call "deliberative ethics, a set of questions that form a 'living code' that can be applied to the ethical dilemmas that arise in various professions."[58]

Obviously, there are many traditions affirmed and explored in a university's curriculum, and many professors and administrators, personally and professionally, quarrel with the predominance of student ambitions to get a job and make a buck that any kind of credential supposedly offers. But in the desire to attract and retain as many students as possible, most of the recruitment literature and amenities of colleges and universities promote career development, not moral development. What the student wants has become the measure, rather than what the student may owe others. Moral development is easily neglected when an institution's "competition" ignores it and the bottom line is institutional advancement, or even survival. For those embedded in America's culture of professionalism, whatever moral sensibilities seem lacking have, strangely enough, been replaced by considering competence as a contemporary form of virtue. I have written elsewhere that

> It is understandable why so many professionals treat competence as a virtue—the professional enterprise leaves so little room for anything else. Their gifts and talents, opinions and sentiments not subject to professional measure are largely ignored. . . . The problem, however, of treating competence as a virtue is that competence is really *not* a virtue at all. When we say that virtue is its own reward, we mean that any virtue, such as courage, honesty, or [doing] justice, properly understood and appreciated, is an end in itself. But professional competence, properly understood and appreciated, has only instrumental value; it is meant to serve as a means to other ends. If you make competence a virtue, an end in itself, you have no grounds for finally determining the value of what you know or do, or for evaluating what others know or do.[59]

When competence is combined with a credential, the temptation is to put aside the traditional notion of professional service as a "calling" and substitute "I hear $ calling." "The modern professions have enjoyed their monopoly for so long that they have forgotten that it is a privilege given in exchange for a public benefit." And Jacques Barzun went on to say: "The tendency of an egalitarian age to turn every occupation into a profession has complicated the substance of ethics."[60] Barzun made those observations some thirty-five years ago. What would he make of America's culture of professionalism now? The culture has allowed almost anyone with a credential to posture himself as a professional and exploit those who assume their interests will come before those who profess to serve them. In academe, peer oversight polices competence among colleagues sharing the same discipline, but professionals in practice do not necessarily experience such peer oversight, and clients often cannot judge competence. Most clients willingly yield to those whose esoteric knowledge is beyond their understanding or whose tacit knowledge is beyond their experience. Furthermore, the pretension of professionals seemingly knowing more than they actually do sometimes makes them resemble magicians, despite the observation of Laurence Veysey that experts in the United States have been "far less consistently trusted than were the sorcerers of other times and places, but half a charm has proved better than none."[61] Ralph Waldo Emerson once exclaimed, as was his habit in rhetorical overreaching: "The world is his who can see through its pretension," but that is beyond most everyone in this modern day whether layperson or credentialed specialist given the modern division of mental labor.[62] Bernie Ronan at Maricopa Community College in Phoenix, Arizona, struck a fair balance when he told me: "We all want answers; we strive for certainty. We look to professionals to give it to us. Good professionals should couch their answers with the boundedness that is required by the uncertainty of the universe, however unsettling it might be to the listener."[63]

Nonetheless, the experience in academe conditions both would-be professionals and those who do not entertain such ambitions to accept a false premise that those in the know must look after those who are not qualified, with the have-nots ignoring their own unused capacities in favor of becoming dependent on those who are credentialed. As a consequence, those credentialed, who are seeking status and substantial income, too often create dependence rather than nurturing the capacities of those they ostensibly serve. As John McKnight once put it: "The client is less a person in need than a person who is needed."[64] As a matter of history, Samuel Haber argues: "The tradesman and artisans gave their customers what they wanted. The professional gave his clients and patients what he thought was good for them."[65]

Consider the examples of professional politicians and public servants. I once came across an advertisement for a graduate school of political management that headlined "Professional Politics Isn't for Amateurs." Nothing could be more obvious—acquire professional skills or else stay on the sidelines while those who know better do the social problem solving for you. Nothing, however, could be more misleading than the proposition that the public world rightfully belongs to professionals. Academe often promotes a similarly skewed vision, but nothing could be more self-serving than to put "public service" on the shelf beyond the reach of the lay public. It comes back to how would-be professionals are educated by the example of professors yielding to colleagues on all matters not within their areas of specialization. It hardly encourages students to develop the habit of seeking knowledge outside of their field, and as citizens they may very well forfeit the opportunities to be active participants across a wide spectrum of public issues.

Young men and women need more than *training* to use an "analytic mind" within a specialized field. They deserve an *education* that helps them develop an "inquiring mind." Too many of them are currently schooled to assume that the problems offered in a classroom have been perfected by instructors before being offered for solution. But perfect problems and perfect answers are a serious distortion of what actually goes on in social problem solving, whether in government or the communities where they will live. To practice their skills in a classroom where problems come ready-made with enormous amounts of data does not prepare them to be inquiring citizens who construct as best they can, with or without professional help, the kind of trial-and-error processes in which most civic learning is grounded. Similarly, as students they may fail to develop a "strategic mind" nourished by experiencing both inside and outside the classroom what it means to get out of themselves and "into the other person's shoes." They are handicapped not only by normal egocentricity but also by the mistaken belief, fostered on many occasions by professors, of insisting on "objective" analysis of a problem situation without regard for how the problem appears subjectively to others. After students have been outfitted with a host of problem-solving methodologies, they may neglect the simple approach of finding out what others know and want, instead relying on this objective analysis or that methodology. Students may learn that right answers are enough when taking an exam, but it is not likely to be enough in the real world where many "answers" compete and conflict.

"A Bunch of Amateurs" (I)

Nathan Sax, the president of Pennacook University, looked out the window from his office in Bancroft Hall. There they were on a bright September morning, 75 students walking back and forth with signs saying, "Divest Now: Fossil-Fuels Make Climate-Fools," and chanting, "Facts, facts, Dr. Sax, sell the stock or get the axe."

Sax didn't like the chant, but he knew where it came from. *Campus Citizen*, the student newspaper, had written a scathing editorial denouncing the president "for studying the divestment question to death. Even in academia, dear Nathan, there is a limit to how long you can examine an issue." From his window, Sax could see some younger faculty members talking with the milling students. Certain factions in the faculty were also "fed up" with Sax, according to the *Campus Citizen*.

Sax turned away from the window. He knew that the divestment question would be the major item on the Board of Trustees' agenda when it met later in the week. The students were right, of course—Nathan Sax was slow to act. He had always believed that reasoned deliberation was the only appropriate style for a university president. There were so many people to talk to, so many meetings, so many committees. And besides, Sax was convinced that divestment was not the "climate change" issue that the students portrayed it to be. Colorful rhetoric, yes, but he was rarely moved by rhetoric. The university was too embedded in a history and a city with priorities that did not agree with the opinions and demands of students who made their home at Pennacook for four years and then moved out, moved on.

Looking out the window again, Sax thought social critic Paul Goodman was about right when he said, "The young are lively, beautiful and callous . . . and there is nothing to do but love them. If this is impossible, the next best thing is to resent them." This morning Nathan Sax resented them, especially after consulting again with Pennacook's investment adviser, Harry Frank, who Sax thought was a first-rate professional, and whose advice he and the board normally followed. It was Frank who told Sax, "What do these kids know? The financial cost of Pennacook divesting itself of investments based on criteria other than expected performance would very likely be substantial. And it would not include the substantial transaction costs that Pennacook would incur by divesting part of its portfolio. I'm telling you, Nathan, you can't afford to listen to a bunch of amateurs."

The president reviewed in his mind the events of the past six months. A coalition of student groups advocating divestment, Students for Divestment Now (SDN), launched a "spring offensive," protesting the failure of the university to sell all the stock it owned in fossil-fuel companies. SDN had prevailed upon the student senate to withdraw $50,000 of its funds, which was part of the university's investment pool, and instead put the money in a Renewable Energy and Sustainability Fund.

As Sax stared out the window, Sonya Manka, the university's vice president for finance, came in. Manka had never been sympathetic to the SDN cause and, time and again, advised Sax to stick to the independent and objective advice of Harry Frank and other "professionals" on the trustee board. As far as Manka was concerned, "endowments and investments should never be used as political tools. Besides, fossil-fuel companies are dependable profit generators." Joining Sax at the window, Manka squinted. "Well," she said, "they're at it again and just in time for another trustees' meeting. I don't understand why they think divestment is a persuasive tactic with American companies. There are plenty of smart buyers of stock who are less interested in divestment than the few who sell. Divestment by Pennacook won't change a thing." Manka turned away from the window. "So many of the students are such hypocrites. They don't call for a ban on campus recruiting by those same companies. They are always badgering somebody else to do something."

Sax turned to Manka, "I'm not a lawyer, but our counsel advises me that as long as the trustees take no action that is contrary to public policy, they will be indemnified. Anyway, who is going to sue them?"

"Me," Sonya said emphatically and then laughed. "That is if our portfolio gets messed up by selling off some of our strongest equities. You know as well as I do that since the Great Recession, a strong, recovering performance of our endowment remains absolutely critical to keeping this place afloat."

The president liked Manka despite her heated opinions. He badly needed her expertise in disciplining a budget that was vulnerable to the annual competition for student enrollments, the unending demands of maintenance on buildings that were far beyond their useful life, faculty always seeking higher salaries, and the wage demands of Pennacook's unionized staff.

"You've heard it before from Harry Frank. 'Don't give in to a bunch of amateurs.'" Manka glanced again at the students outside and then promptly left.

Nathan Sax was soon off to consult with Francis Moody, the board chair, at Moody's office in the First State Bank downtown, but first he wanted to visit with the demonstrators outside. As he was leaving, his assistant, Tim Delroy, stopped him to report that SDN had requested the Pennacook alumni list for a mailing.

"What kind of mailing?" Sax asked.

"They didn't say. I have heard, however, that they want to discourage contributions to annual giving until the trustees act favorably on divestment. The SDN also wants the alumni to join them in getting the board to enlarge its membership to include pro-divestment students, faculty and alums."

Sax groaned. "That would be an awful precedent. The trustees will never buy that, never."

"Do we give them the list?" Tim asked.

"I don't see how we can refuse them." Sax headed for the door. "Tim, I'm going out to see the students, then downtown for Francis Moody."

Delroy held the door for the president. "Do you really want to debate the SDN this early in the day?"

"Better outside now than having them sitting in my office when I get back." Sax walked out into the glare and blare of the September demonstration.

After years of teaching philosophy, Nathan Sax had developed the Socratic habit of playful, and sometimes not so playful, debate on whatever issue students confronted him with. It often got him in trouble, however, when Pennacook students, soberly engaged in an important cause, became infuriated with his seeming detachment. Sax tried to adjust his style but old habits die hard. As Sax walked toward the students, the chanting stopped and several of them walked quickly over to see him.

"Have you decided to move the trustee meeting off campus? We heard that . . ."

Sax cut them off. "I've heard no such thing. No, the trustees will meet where they always do, in the Curtis Room of Bancroft Hall."

The students now surrounded him. He looked at each student in the circle. He did not know many of them by name but he recognized some and nodded in a friendly way. They smiled and nodded back. A few remained sullen.

One young man spoke up: "Dr. Sax, we'd like to know what your recommendation will be to the trustees." The others nodded in agreement.

"Who says I'm to make a recommendation? I didn't know the trustees needed my recommendation. They are quite able to act on their own, you know."

Jenny Stackhouse, whom Sax had met with once before, raised her hand, then laughed at the gesture and moved to the president's side. "Dr. Sax, we just want you to care, for the trustees to care, for Pennacook to care about what's going on with climate change."

Sax turned to her. "What makes you think that we don't care? I'm surprised you think that we don't . . ."

Stackhouse persisted. "You don't care enough to make a sacrifice, if that's what divestment means to you."

Sax looked at the other students. "I'm sorry but I don't understand why my caring for Pennacook, trying to avoid unnecessary costs, trying to keep your tuition within reason . . ." Some students started to hiss. Sax went on. "What we care about can be a very complicated business. My job is to . . ."

"Your job is to lead," another student edged closer, "Your job, to follow your logic, is to make us care about this university, and you can't do that if you put dollars ahead of saving the planet."

"I hear you," Sax said, looking at the student. "Is our decision here at Pennacook meant to be effective or symbolic?"

"Both," many students said in unison. "Both, Dr. Sax."

Jenny Stackhouse resumed her argument. "It is the right thing to do." Her eyes glistened. "It shows that we care, that you care, Dr. Sax, that the trustees care."

Sax thought she was starting over again. He couldn't stop himself. "Caring, all right the subject is caring. Let me ask you if we were talking about companies that are important to this town or provide jobs for people who live here, would you still say that we should divest?"

The students looked at each other. They didn't understand Sax's question. "C'mon doctor, that's a hypothetical, a red herring. What companies in this town will be hurt if Pennacook divests?"

"I don't know," and Sax really didn't know, but he had made the argument and now he felt compelled to continue. "But if they were, would you care if it meant people lost their jobs?"

"No," one student said emphatically. "When it comes to climate change, everyone has to pay their dues."

Sax thought he saw an opening. "Oh, I'm sure they're willing to pay their dues," he looked intently at the student, "they just don't want to pay yours." The students hissed again and started to drift away.

Sax started walking and a few students followed along to ask more questions about what would happen at the trustees' meeting. Sax could hear them chant again. "Facts, Facts, Dr. Sax!" He had said too much or not said enough. When he reached the campus gates, the students turned back and he stopped momentarily to make some notes. "Next time," he vowed, "I won't use any hypothetical."

PART II

Culture Change?

CHAPTER 4

Nobody's Property

America's culture of professionalism, which emerged in the late nineteenth century and ascended in the twentieth, largely treated knowledge as a form of property secured by a necessary credential. Possession gave knowledge production a market value. Today, however, knowledge as a social construct is emerging from a variety of collaborative learning sources that go beyond what academics and professionals have secured with their peers. Without professional guidance, there is an end run around proprietary knowledge by different forms of networking unimagined only a few generations ago. David Weinberger, senior researcher at Harvard's Berkman Center for Internet and Society, argues: "Individuals thinking out loud now have weight, and authority and expertise are losing some of their gravity."[1]

Weinberger refers to "social knowing," which he describes as knowledge that "isn't in our heads: It is between us."[2] There are social networks and various support groups that offer new forms of self-help as part of far-flung movements of knowledge sharing and belonging. David Weinberger points out that "knowledge—its content and its organization—is becoming a social act." In a rapidly changing world, "customers, patrons, users, and citizens are not waiting for permission to take control of finding and organizing information."[3] Weinberger, however, glosses over the difference between information and knowledge. When two people exchange information online, it does not necessarily amount to sharing knowledge. This often means that professionals who are in-the-know have the advantage over laypersons, but, beyond the limited boundaries of their expertise, professionals can be as ignorant as anyone else. In any event, treating knowledge as a social construct is becoming far more accessible without strict boundaries between those who are credentialed and those who are not.

Collaborative Learning

Sources of collaborative learning are found wherever there are opportunities for online learning, when strangers come together to share what they know and what they seek to know; wherever there are classroom learning circles that assume a rough equality between students and their teachers; and wherever there is social learning from *experience* whether gained from classroom practicums, community educators, or just plain everyday life. This is not an exhaustive list, but I have chosen sources that do not fit neatly in the current culture of professionalism. Collaborative learning is often part of a nonhierarchical social process shared by equals. Such relative equality does not assume equal talent, but it does assume equal access to whatever those involved can learn together.

Self-reliance can be a distracting legacy when so much of our social existence now depends, more than ever, on finding ways to sort out mutual interests. Economic theory has doted on individual capacity with far less attention paid to social contexts with which individual capacity must struggle to understand and come to terms. This is one reason rational decision theory is being contested by behavioral economics, which does more to acknowledge social complexity. "Social complexity has us moving from the 'me' perspective to the 'we' perspective."[4] There is a line of American thinkers—Oliver Wendell Holmes, William James, and John Dewey, among others, who "believed that ideas are not produced by individuals—that ideas are social."[5] Citing Dewey's work, Albert Dzur puts it this way: "Social intelligence" accounts for what people develop together "not the private intelligence of think tanks and policy experts."[6] Treating knowledge as a social construct is, of course, what credentialed specialists do in academe or elsewhere among their peers, but in a culture of professionalism most specialists do not think to include individuals without credentials.

I should acknowledge here that Kenneth Bruffee's important work on collaborative learning has helped to shape my thinking about treating knowledge as a social construct.[7] There is nothing complicated about the practice of collaborative learning, but it does undermine those who assert the authority of their knowledge and their position in an organizational hierarchy whether in academe or elsewhere. Despite the habits of peer sharing with colleagues in academe, knowledge as a social construct, emerging from a variety of collaborative learning sources, does not require professional credentials to be valued and shared, and it does mean giving up any semblance of control.[8] Such control has always been an attractive advantage, but Bruffee challenged the status quo, arguing, like John Dewey, that collaborative learning makes teachers *and* students "the chief carriers of control," and "changing what teachers do implies changing what they think knowledge is."[9] Consequently, collaborative learning can be an enormous challenge to the professional mind-set. Can professors share with their students what they share with their peer colleagues? If peer sharing assumes that one's colleagues are qualified, then extending the same respect to students, who are not as proficient, would seem inconsistent. Nonetheless, Bruffee thinks "mature, effective interdependence—that is, social maturity integrated with intellectual maturity—may be the most important lesson students should be asked to learn."[10] When graduates move on from academe, their collaborative learning experience may help shape their expectations and performance online, in organizations, and in community life. Collaborative habits are likely to foster a working equality in the variety of settings that they encounter.

Bruffee recognized that collaborative learning is essential among various peer groups in academe, pointing to Thomas Kuhn's oft-cited work, *The Structure of Scientific Revolutions*. Kuhn's landmark study examined the "paradigms" and "pivots" of scientific research. For Kuhn: "Scientific knowledge, like language, is intrinsically the common property of a group or nothing at all."[11] More recently David Weinberger acknowledged Kuhn's enormous influence on how we think about those who "do" science. Weinberger points out that such knowledge arises "within a social realm of social striving, personal interests, shared hopes," despite the long-standing authority of credentialed institutions that have promoted "the illusion of near-uniform assent."[12] And James Surowiecki has noted that "although in the popular imagination, science remains the province of the lone genius working alone in the lab, in fact, it is, in more ways than one, a profoundly collective experience."[13] There are also many new outlets online where scientists can share what they know or what they want to learn more about. ResearchGate, a social networking site for scientists, is one example. It is a platform for housing abstracts and papers. Although 2.9 million researchers are already using it, Dr. Ijad Madisch of ResearchGate conceded that it has not been used by many established scientists. "But wait" he says, "until younger scientists weaned on social media and open-source collaboration start running their own labs."[14]

The *diversity* of minds engaged in collaborative learning can also be important. James Surowiecki's *The Wisdom of Crowds* made popular the idea that the more participants the better, but with a caveat that the diversity of those participating is essential.[15] Scott Page argues that "gathering together the best and brightest minds . . . that's a flawed approach. We also need to pay attention to the diversity of those minds, all the more so if the old saying that 'great minds think alike' holds true."[16] No doubt, there are increasing numbers of commentators, some of whom I cite in this chapter, who sit somewhere between the academic rigor of Page's work and Surowiecki's popularization of collaborative learning. What Surowiecki and Page have in common is a certainty that the production of knowledge has far fewer boundaries and far more sources than it once did. A diversity of minds working together, however, cannot be taken for granted, given the attraction of niche media and websites that reinforce, rather than challenge, the polarization of opinion on social issues.

Collaborative learning assumes a democratic setting whether in a classroom, a workplace, or a community meeting place. Such settings, however, often do not offer collaborative learning opportunities among equals. As two seeming mavericks in academe, Paul Markham and Eric Bain-Selbo, argue: "How can we expect students to develop the skills and capacities of civic life and be trained in democratic processes if they are part of institutions that are authoritarian, hierarchical, and increasingly run like a corporation in which faculty are merely employees and students merely consumers?"[17] It follows then that the practice of collaborative learning is perhaps the most promising social process to mitigate the damage being done in academe by well-meaning but short-sighted instruction; by workplaces with an executive hierarchy that maintains traditional forms of top-down management; and by public servants and experts who treat citizens in community meetings as a deserving *audience* in need of professional help. Too often in such settings "inquiry, discovery, and co-creation" is given no room to take root and grow.[18] In a recent lecture, William Bowen, former president of Princeton, cited Jacob Viner: "There is no limit to the amount of nonsense you can think, if you think alone."[19] *Others* create problems for us and *others* are needed to solve them. And what *others* do in solving or not solving them helps to determine what we do. There are endless examples of how our lives have become more complicated but better served by collaborative learning. As William Sullivan observed, "individual lives have become ever more intricately tied into unseen networks of interdependence."[20] Collaborative learning assumes that there is a willing *interdependence* among those who have something to learn from each other. Learning, too often, is portrayed as someone burning the midnight oil by oneself when, in fact, most learning occurs when people put their heads together; and in this day and age when many, many heads collaborate online. I have written elsewhere that "interdependence, not community, is the more reliable concept for explaining how we now live together."[21] Zagat publications provide a commercial example of such collaboration. Zagat does not rely on expert food critics for restaurant reviews, it relies on aggregating the opinions of ordinary diners. Zagat has always believed "that the collective opinions of knowledgeable consumers are more accurate than the opinions of a single critic."[22] John McKnight makes a similar distinction: "A self-organizing group is built and focused on people's gifts, whereas a managed system is built and focused on needs."[23]

Michael Schrage at the MIT Media Lab examined what drives innovation among those in private enterprise, and he discovered that it was social interactions among relative equals. Rather than relying on predetermined design in an organization, innovation evolves among such equals. Innovation fares best as a social process among those intent on learning together without any "aha" moment of discovery. Individuals seeking to innovate require little oversight and direction from people with authority who lack the requisite knowledge to foresee or shape the innovation. Schrage describes innovation in business as "a culture that places a premium on active participation."[24] Consider a McKinsey and Company study in 2012 that "found the use of social networking within companies increased the productivity of 'knowledge workers' by 20 to 25%."[25]

Those in academe, of course, have not ignored the new sources of collaborative learning that have emerged. Twenty years ago in a study titled "The New Production of Knowledge," six scholars from different continents and disciplines sought to explain changes in how knowledge was produced, what they call "Mode 2" as opposed to the traditional "Mode 1" in academe. Far from trying to write a trade book, their treatise stayed comfortably on the dense academic side of the street, but with an intelligent respect for the unending potential of Mode 2. They did not choose sides and thought that the two modes were "simply different."[26] They observed that Mode 1 is "hierarchical" while Mode 2 "is more heterarchical and transient." Mode 1 is "disciplinary" while Mode 2 is "transdisciplinary." Mode 1 is "characterized by homogeneity, Mode 2 by heterogeneity" with "an increase in the number of potential sites where knowledge can be created." In Mode 2, they saw research groups as less "institutionalized: people come together in temporary work teams and networks," which dissolve "when a problem is solved or redefined."[27] The authors noted that Mode 2 lacks the peer control of Mode 1 as well as its controlling mechanisms and hierarchies. They did, however, point out that Mode 2 entertains a greater range of criteria for examining the value of what knowledge is produced. As an emerging "group phenomenon," they described Mode 2 as a "socially distributed knowledge product system."[28]

Like so many in academe, the co-authors of the study spoke of "advances" in science and technology—the assumption being of an expected linear progression. "Advances" is an interesting and revealing word choice that reflects the traditional optimism that knowledge production, if not unerring, is at least moving in the right direction. For some in academe, knowledge is the discovery of something with an independent existence; for others, knowledge has no such preexisting standing and can only be affirmed, and then only temporarily, by those who brought it into existence. Gerald Graff pointed out the "mutual smugness" in academe of those who hold to a "concept of objectivity and the extent to which knowledge is independent of the social situation of the knower," and "revisionists," who don't.[29]

Networked Learning Online

Let me say at the outset that this part of the discussion on collaborative learning is not about the online teaching and learning that so many academic institutions and for-profit enterprises are pursuing.[30] Online instruction is a subject that deserves and is receiving increasing attention, but it is primarily an exciting means of delivering academe's knowledge; my argument here is about the growing presence and potential of collaborative learning online *beyond* academe's offerings. Joichi Ito, the director of the MIT Media Lab, goes so far as to opine that education is not "about centralized instruction anymore; rather, it is the process of establishing oneself as a node in a broad network of distributed creativity."[31] Ito sees that such learning is a welcome and important option for those who cannot afford or do not have access to what academe has to offer.

Too often the world beyond academe is slighted or ignored. Education in America, as the historian Lawrence Cremin so thoroughly and eloquently described, has had many sources beyond schools or academe. Twenty-five years ago, Cremin saw that "new technologies" were "providing incomparable opportunities for teaching and learning that completely bypassed schools and colleges and go directly into the household."[32] Now online networks go way beyond any geographical boundaries and redefine where some "communities" actually reside. Networked learning online may or may not lead to the social construction of knowledge, but such learning is what almost anyone can pursue. For David Weinberger "knowledge is now a property of the network," not just treated as such in academe and professional practice, "and the network embraces business, governments, media, museums, curated collections, and minds in communication."[33] By "minds in communication," Weinberger presumably means everyone who has reason to learn from others. Although Weinberger describes knowledge as property, it can belong to a far wider circle online with "expertise . . . moving from being property of individual experts to becoming property of the Net."[34] The elaborate use of hyperlinks is evidence that any particular knowledge source is not necessarily a sufficient destination.[35] For those who want to learn online, rather than just shop there to consume, there are many complicated journeys to pursue. One virtue of an amateur is that he can pursue an interesting path for its own sake and find others along that path, which often makes it a more worthwhile journey.

If networked learning online does not currently pose a threat to those with credentialed knowledge, it does provide various new avenues for learning without necessarily challenging what is already known. This method of learning allows an infinite number of users to better understand what is already known or is still in development, and, when so many people are gaining access to knowledge properties, such learning may very well begin to challenge the culture of professionalism. Those who "trespass" may or may not be interested in reshaping or qualified to alter knowledge properties, but they are likely to affect how the "owners" look after and tend their properties and with whom they collaborate to improve them. As a consequence, knowledge as a form of property will lose some of its exclusivity and become more a "common ground" for those interested in cultivating it, instead of being an exclusive domain for "peers" who have so far been its caretakers.

Networked learning online certainly helps students better understand why treating knowledge as a possession misconstrues the wired world they now live in. Their professors, of course, already know that knowledge is really a social construct with their peers. When students bring along to their classrooms whatever learning they have acquired from an abundance of online sources, they may not so much compete with as complement what their courses offer. Faculty and institutions that try to ignore or condescend to such student contributions run the risk of being ignored or condescended to in return. Students from generation to generation have tended to adapt and imitate, as best they could, the academic priorities and style of their professors. Looking ahead, however, students who use networked learning online as a supplement to their passage through academe may very well change the hierarchical and antidemocratic setting they find there. For better or worse, depending on where you stand or sit in academe, syllabi and the conduct of courses will be affected.

Of course, there are skeptics and critics of the value and so-called promise of networked learning online. One outspoken critic is Nicholas Carr, whose *The Shallows: What the Internet Is Doing to Our Brains* stands out in unapologetic opposition to the many more positive and sometimes over-the-top celebrations of what the Internet era has wrought. Carr sees the Internet as luring "thoughtful people to slip comfortably into the permanent state of distractedness . . . we have rejected the intellectual tradition of solitary, single-minded concentration, the ethic that the book bestowed on us. We have cast our lot with the juggler."[36] Carr, however, seems to assume an either/or learning environment, which is not necessarily accurate. Even Carr admits it may be a trade-off: "We gain new skills and perspectives and lose old ones."[37] What is not clear is why Carr thinks most Americans supposedly prefer the Internet to traditional sources of learning, such as reading books. Reading goes on in many different venues, including online, and quality is measured by what a source offers not by what the source is. Anyone who has used Google knows how vast that database is and how much information and knowledge can be quickly gleaned.

Andrew Keen is another critic with a different slant in the midst of the abundant literature celebrating the Internet. Keen takes to the "professional" barricades seeing the "ubiquity of free user-generated content" as threatening "the very core of our professional institutions."[38] Keen goes even further: "The arbiters of truth should be the experts—those who speak from a place of knowledge—not the winners of a popularity contest."[39] It is surprising, however, that an entrepreneur like Keen looks down on the digital herds. Networked learning online is not so much a truth-seeking journey as it is a modest, but more important, site of collaboration with those who share similar topics and concerns. Keen chooses to ignore the capacities of citizens in favor of the supposed certainties entertained in America's culture of professionalism.

Susan Cain, who is generally critical of various forms of what she calls "groupthink," makes an exception for networked learning online when she says "large groups outperform individuals . . . It's a place where we can be alone together—and this is what gives it power."[40] Like democracy, networked learning online has no fixed destination—it is a social process that invites participation but with no guarantee what it may produce. However, Mathew Hindman, skeptical about "digital democracy," warns: "We must be mindful of the difference between speaking and being heard."[41] Hindman understands, as many others do, that social media encourages anyone and everyone to have their say, but too easily assume that everyone or anyone is listening. Nonetheless, Howard Rheingold, a technology guru, offered his succinct summary of the value of various networks: "When a network is aimed at broadcasting something of value to individuals . . . the value of service is linear. When the network enables transactions between the individual nodes, the value is squared. When the same network includes ways for individuals to form groups, the value is exponential."[42]

"Open source" is an important network process that rejects knowledge as a form of property and throws open the doors to qualified contributors. Eric Raymond, another technology guru, explained that Linus Torvalds's debugging of the Linux operating system evolved "by the naively simple strategy of releasing every week and getting feedback from hundreds of users within days."[43] Torvalds's open source was a learning process that existed not for the sake of those who contributed, but nonetheless offered everyone the opportunity to learn something. Open source has migrated from its Linux origins by treating knowledge as a social construct without proprietary assumptions. Whose "property" is it anyway when it comes to networked sharing and learning online? Political science professor Steven

Weber argues: "Open source radically inverts the core notion of property" stretching its meaning, at least online, to "the right to distribute, not the right to exclude."[44] Professor of law Jedediah Purdy, however, thinks the core notion of property remains a significant obstacle: "Our dominant vision of property as a matter of exclusive rights applied to all valuable resources may stand in the way of fully realizing the potential of a digital era."[45] Although intellectual property and the licensing of software remain prominent, open source has maintained its presence as an attractive alternative. For example, the PatientsLikeMe website serves as a source for those wanting to learn from those with similar chronic medical conditions.[46] Such networked learning online ignores the existing norm that one's medical data is a private matter. Sharing medical information is the whole point of a collaborative site where the learning potential usually exceeds any value of withholding one's medical history.[47] Another interesting use of open source has been the health industry's harvesting of information from "health consumers," thereby influencing health treatments and products.[48] So, one way or another, open source technologies have fostered an "architecture of participation" in a wide range of organizations.[49]

Those who engage in open source projects often bring with them a *reputation* of one kind or another, which often affects how well their respective contributions are accepted by others.[50] Reputation is especially important online when others have little else to go on when sharing a project. One's reputation, however, is not something everyone else may be familiar with, but it can be established by how one contributes to a particular collaborative learning project. It can take some time to establish, but once one's reputation is clarified collaboration among strangers has some grounding. Reputation building is similar to what those in academe pursue or evaluate when sharing what they have developed in their respective fields. Reputation becomes a necessary currency, not just knowledge in development.

And then there is crowdsourcing, a process used increasingly by businesses to enlarge their input for developing new products. Crowdsourcing is less concerned with the social construction of knowledge than it is in uncovering "existing knowledge, thus simplifying the discovery capabilities of an organization with limited resources."[51] Nonprofit organizations and government agencies also use this top-down, bottom-up process to enlarge their base of knowledge about whatever they seek to develop, by leveraging "the collective intelligence of online communities to serve specific organizational goals."[52] The degree to which credentialed professionals predominate and control input distinguishes crowdsourcing from open source enterprises. These professionals seek a measure of control over *how* knowledge is produced, not just *what* is produced. Nonetheless, Daren Brabham at the University of North Carolina's School of Journalism and Mass Communication notes: "Crowds and the low-cost, high-quality creative work they produce threaten the very notion of professionalism."[53]

Journalist Chris Anderson captured the essence of networked learning online as follows: "Now we're depending more and more on systems where nobody's in charge; the intelligence is simply 'emergent.'" For Anderson, the value of the "world of 'peer production' . . . of mass volunteerism and amateurism" is by no means settled, but "people are re-forming into thousands of cultural *tribes of interest,* connected less by geographic proximity and workplace chatter than by shared interests."[54] For Clay Shirky, an expert observer of the Internet phenomenon, : "We are all living through the disorientation that comes from including two billion new participants in a media landscape previously operated by a small group of professionals."[55] For David Weinberger: "We get to create our own categories, ones that suit our way of thinking. Experts can be helpful, but in the age of miscellaneous they and their institutions are no longer in charge of our ideas."[56]

How does this all affect academe—the home office of professionalism? Will networked learning online require a reassessment of proprietary expertise? When I asked this of an associate professor of higher education, she said, "the networking of knowledge requires us to consider what university folks uniquely bring to a knowledge problem. Is it talent? Or academic skills? Clearly it is not control over knowledge, as the trend is to greater democracy on knowledge access and production. I think our unique contribution might . . . relate to how we can attract talents and use certain skills to bring partners together to solve problems."[57] When I asked the same question of a professor of communication studies, he saw a significant impact on how higher education should function: "The importance of learning basic knowledge and memorizing facts significantly decreases, and the [importance] of how to process information and how to make good judgments significantly increases."[58] Credentials often seem far removed from those collaborating online. Like a potluck dinner, not served up by one credentialed chef in control of the menu, whatever people bring to the table is consumed by those who feast on the variety and abundance of what others have chosen to share together. At the table, what is shared belongs to no one in particular. Like the potluck dinner, networked learning online delivers and consumes knowledge that is nobody's property.

Classroom Learning Circles

Kenneth Bruffee argues that "collaborative learning tasks . . . do not presuppose either one right answer or one acceptable method for arriving at it."[59] Bruffee cites James Coleman, the sociologist, who thought that it was through "collaborative activities that adolescents are more effectively drawn into active participation in academic and other constructive activities."[60] Bruffee sees that collaborative learning helps students understand that "knowledge is not a universal entity but a local one, constructed and maintained by local consensus and subject to endless conversation."[61] How very different that is from the traditional presentation by many of those in academe who deliver knowledge from a lectern for their students' benefit. Sitting in a classroom learning circle that includes the professor can establish a rough equality among the group as opposed to an auditorium or lecture hall where the professor presides over those attending. For the sociologist Parker Palmer: "If we regard truth as something handed down from authorities on high, the classroom will look like a dictatorship . . . If we regard truth as emerging from a complex process of mutual inquiry, the discussion will look like a resourceful and interdependent community."[62]

A classroom learning circle does not follow a linear path toward a designated goal laid out by those with authority and knowledge. It is much more complicated than that. In learning circles there are no predetermined best choices that exist independently of those taking part. Educators can help young people learn to shape their own choices when together they identify issues, frame them, and decide how to proceed. Whatever choices emerge are not prescribed by anyone, but instead evolve in the learning circle. Unfortunately, most formal schooling does not offer or encourage this style of learning. Some teachers fear a loss of control. They take for granted that what they know and want to convey is far superior to what they think students know. They too often neglect the educator role, preferring the more limited role of delivering information and knowledge that their students can use for test taking. Working together in learning circles can help young people understand that learning is an ongoing process, not a delivered product—more a social phenomenon than just a cognitive task. There is no hierarchy in a learning circle and those in a circle cannot turn their backs on anyone who is part of it. Political science professor Charles Anderson would say: "The object is really not that students should 'think for themselves.' Rather, knowing is common and collaborative. For understanding to advance, we must think alike and we must also think differently, but, above all, we must think together."[63] Learning circles, however, are not easily constructed and maintained. Parker Palmer argues that "opening a learning space requires more skill and more authority than filling it up."[64] Small classes help, as humanities professor Andrew Delbanco has observed, where the teacher "is neither oracle nor lawgiver but a kind of provocateur."[65] Learning circles are some distance from literary theorist and legal scholar Stanley Fish's assumption that "the true task of academic work [is] the search for truth and the dissemination of it through teaching."[66] Note who does the searching as far as Fish is concerned.

In K-12 education there are some interesting examples of classroom learning circles. They include two academies that are worlds apart—Exeter, a leading preparatory school in New Hampshire, and The New American Academy, an elementary school serving disadvantaged kids in Crown Heights, Brooklyn. What they have in common are learning circles to encourage collaboration among students and their teachers. David Brooks, op-ed columnist for *The New York Times,* observed: "Like Phillips Exeter Academy, [New American Academy] students are less likely to sit at individual desks than around big tables."[67] The New American Academy is designed to be a learning organization "using four-person teaching teams under the leadership of a "Master Teacher." Students learn "to explore the world around them through collaborative inquiry and an interdisciplinary curriculum, which employs small group activity and peer-to-peer learning." Brooks thinks "The New American Academy has the potential to create richer mentorlike or even familylike relationships for students who are not rich in those things."[68] Similar "academies" are opening elsewhere in New York City.

The Harkness Table at Phillips Exeter Academy has been a learning circle practice for more than eighty years. It originated with a gift in 1930 from the philanthropist Edward Harkness. The classroom tables were oval, not round, so everyone at a table could make eye contact. Since an oval table was too big to fit through Exeter's doorways, the tables were constructed inside the classrooms—meaning that "Harkness Tables really are part of the rooms in which Exeter's community learns, teaches, discusses, and collaborates."[69] Since Edward Harkness gave the school $5.8 million, they were able to get it right.

To learn more about the Harkness Table, I reached out to Exeter's principal, Thomas Hassan; Richard Schubart, who recently retired after teaching history at Exeter for many years and leading a study of the Harkness method; two Exeter alums, Wick Sloane, class of 1971, and Isaiah Brown, class of 2012, and Anna Brown, Class of 2014 (the latter two are my grandnephew and grandniece). I asked each of them what they thought were the greatest strengths of the Harkness method. Hassan told me: "Collaborative learning breeds a respect for the opinions of others, and the patience to really listen . . . In some cases it may not be the fastest or most efficient way to impart knowledge, but the fact that students internalize what they learn outweighs this potential shortcoming."[70] And Wick Sloane: "Knowing that the odds are almost 100 percent that you will be called on in class, and often called often, does focus the mind as far as getting homework done. Having that level of accountability become routine at an early age was a benefit."[71] Rick Schubart came right to the point:

> There is no place to hide around the Harkness Table . . . everyone is accountable . . . for formulating effective questions if not answers . . . The Harkness seminar table is. . . . for learning how to learn, where the question one asks of the subject, the assigned text, of one's fellow students, and of oneself are more important than the answer . . . I do wish to emphasize the teaching and learning, and learning and teaching, on the part of both students and faculty. For in my mind the Harkness seminar is ultimately a synergy of both. . . . The good Harkness instructor is one who is passionate about his or her discipline, but realizes that there is always more to learn . . . In sum, teaching and learning at their best are one and the same; both are endless processes, part of the lifelong pursuit of knowledge and goodness, truth and wisdom, culture and civilization.[72]

I recalled Kenneth Bruffee's observation for Schubart that "we tend to forget much of the subject matter" of courses we have taken, but we "don't easily forget the conventions that govern those courses and the values implicit in them."[73] Schubart agreed: "My former Exeter students have put . . . Harkness ideals and principles of practice in all sorts of professional careers from Medicine to Law to Business to Education itself." He went on: "Collaborative decision making in more open forums, as opposed to top-down, hierarchical models, is becoming increasingly the norm in professional life."[74] The "norm" I'm not so sure about, but there is no doubt that collaborative learning can help would-be professionals head in that direction. When I shared Bruffee's observation with Principal Hassam, he referred me to alumni testimony that supported Bruffee. One alum, fifty years out, remembered that "a cornerstone of a Harkness education is vulnerability. There is no retreat for the unprepared, no escape for the uninspired . . . the great teachers use the inherent intimacy that accompanies vulnerability to establish a particular connection with each student. They may even create a subtle, silent link between their students' vulnerability and their own."[75] Only a year out of Exeter, Isaiah Brown added this: "I have found the skills I learned at the table to be valuable in many aspects of my life. It has given me confidence in conversation, taught me to support my arguments with evidence, and to challenge my assumptions."[76] Collaborative learning may frustrate those who think they have the "right" answer or the "correct" method for finding it, although Isaiah put it differently: "The first thing that comes to my mind . . . is Harkness Math: for me math was my favorite Harkness class because it was so different than the way I had learned before. Students took turns sharing solutions they had found to the homework problems and other students helped them if they had gotten stuck or had made a mistake." For Isaiah it was easy to tell who was not prepared and as participation is a large part of the final grade in every class at Exeter there are consequences for those who try to "free ride."[77] His sister Anna had her own experience to share: "If no one corrects an incorrect [answer], some teachers may not say anything for a few days, and see if anyone notices. Even in math, the teacher does not immediately hone down on one correct answer . . . After arriving at an answer, other students will present other ways to get to the same answer. Teachers are especially pleased when a student comes up with a solution that has never before been seen."[78]

Another question I asked was whether networked learning online was a help or a distraction to what went on at a Harkness Table. In answer to my question, Hassan offered a careful distinction: "This digital age . . . poses an exceptional challenge. The means of communicating our thoughts can be much faster than the process of developing meaningful ideas."[79]

Hassan has written elsewhere: "We must consider how our teaching could evolve, in light of the technological tools available to us today and in the future. How can technology enhance our Harkness classrooms without compromising our face-to-face discussion with students?"[80] Isaiah Brown found the frequent use of the Internet at Exeter extended Harkness Table discussions "beyond the walls of the classroom" with some classes having blogs on which students wrote discussion posts as homework.[81]

As for "potluck deliberation" around the Harkness Table, Isaiah Brown remembers: "Students are always expected to bring different contributions to the classroom. This is part of what makes Harkness so successful."[82] Schubart, however, added that "the point is then in general table discussion to see if the greater whole of a thesis can be made from the component parts or multiple pieces of the puzzle."[83] I asked each of them if student writing, as opposed to conversation, allowed more voices to be heard. Anna Brown told me that some students wrote more openly than they spoke in class.[84] Rick Schubart thought that student writing "not only allows more voices to be heard, but the written expression will enhance the verbal contribution, by providing more careful thought and consideration in the preparation and distillation of ideas and opinions . . . Often Harkness classes are asked to write a bit at the beginning of class to clarify thoughts on the subject or topic at hand, and then proceed to discussion."[85] Finally, I asked Schubart what assumptions were critical in the Harkness discussions. He cited three: (1) careful preparation of the text or readings or problems or experiments assigned prior to class, (2) careful listening to one's peers, and (3) consummate respect for one another. He added: "Sometimes too passionate debate or discussion emerges, as they should, and the Harkness Table provides a safe forum for that exchange as long as the assumptions of respectful disagreement and ability to seek an understanding of the opinion opposite is sustained."[86]

Classroom learning circles are also a form of civic education. The civic skills that young people can acquire when working with others in a learning circle include learning to listen—really listen—framing mutual problems, and deliberating together. It is learning to share questions before they can be answered, framing problems before they can be addressed, and sharing options before they can be pursued. All of this takes practice like any skill worth having and using. Such civic education may not be directly relevant to getting a professional credential and employment, but, to the extent learning skills and circle habits begin to be developed in the classrooms, they certainly can be the grounding for an active civic life beyond the classroom. If students cannot be "peers" in knowledge production, they can experience being rough equals with their teachers and professors in the classroom learning circles they come to share. Consequently, three university educators, also working at the K-12 level, see the central purpose of such circles as enabling students to "become active learners, creative real-world problem solvers, and active producers, not simply passive consumers of knowledge."[87]

The experience of being part of classroom learning circles can also help young people realize that deferring to credentialed experts, whose problem-solving processes are rooted in their disciplinary training, too easily excludes the knowledge and experience of everyone else. Instead of just asking a professional what he knows that the questioners don't know, young people can learn to stand that question on its head: "What do we bring to the process that has value? What do we know that he doesn't?" That is why the learning circle experience can lead on to citizen circles in a broader community context. Citizens can move from one circle to another, experiencing their diversity and developing new networks with those willing and able to share their concerns. It takes many circles interacting with each other to get the public's work done, and learning circles explain how collective action may originate and become self-sustaining.

Social Learning from Experience

As noted earlier, "tacit knowledge" has been defined as "a personal skill acquired through practical experience."[88] Such knowledge is an indispensable part of any professional's repertoire. Social learning from experience is much the same. The sociologists Peter Berger and Thomas Luckman had another name for social learning. They called it "common sense knowledge," which is "the knowledge I share with others in the normal, self-evident routines of everyday life."[89] And the popular author Malcolm Gladwell has argued that "social savvy is knowledge," social savvy being another way of describing practical intelligence acquired from experience.[90] I prefer "social learning" to "common sense knowledge" or "social savvy." Social learning captures the process while the others name the result. But each term implies learning from experience so that problems are discovered, not cognitively framed in advance. Experience, which is dynamic rather than static, is a catalyst for learning—adapting, changing, solving problems, or finding new ones. Just thinking about a problem can be too limiting, yielding too few answers.

For social learning experienced in a classroom, social scientist Donald Schon used the term "practicum" for collaborative learning where students learn by *doing*. As Schon put it, "the practicum is a virtual world" with teachers serving as "coaches . . . whose main activities are demonstrating, advising, questioning, and criticizing."[91] In my graduate school teaching, students learned by *doing*, a social experience that I simply called "learning politics." I would begin by telling each student: "If you found yourself on a desert island, there would be no politics. To learn politics is to be engaged in a process of analysis and interaction with other people. Learning politics would begin when you discovered that you were not alone on that desert island; that you were among a strange people in an unfamiliar community. There would be politics, but you would have little chance to be an effective participant until you learned more about where you were." How then could such a conception of politics be brought to life in the classroom? The scaffolding I used consisted of experiential cases that students analyzed and then entered "through the looking glass," so to speak. In other words, each student was given a role from a case to act out. I had found that most teaching cases that students work with do not have a "looking glass" dimension. Students stay outside such cases, analyzing but not participating in their outcomes. They are case histories of other people's decisions in which the students are often no more than disinterested spectators. So the "looking glass" cases that I wrote incorporated three experiences. First, there was the *analytic* experience, constrained by inadequate time and information, during which students sorted out and examined an array of unfamiliar facts and options. Next, there was the *interactive* experience of making decisions or producing outcomes with other role players in the case. Students then had the opportunity to compare the analytic experience of what they anticipated they would do with the interactive experience of what they actually did. Finally, there was the *consequential* experience of analyzing and living with the effects of the decisions or outcomes of their role-playing exercise. The consequential experience did not mean just a debriefing in class to examine why their analyses and interactions worked or did not work. A "looking glass" case offered subsequent episodes in which students traced and reacted to the consequences of their earlier decisions. These "layered" cases were continuous stories that grew more complex but also assumed that students were becoming more politically adept through their increasing familiarity with the social context in which they found themselves. The "looking glass" experience became the necessary scaffolding for dramatizing the observation that learning politics is a shared experience.

Social learning from experience was also of interest to Charles Lindblom, who argued that experiencing a problem in everyday life is often a precondition for doing something about it. "If people do not feel an aversion to a situation or state of affairs, they cannot formulate it as a problem."[92] More than thirty years ago, Lindblom and David Cohen authored *Usable Knowledge*, which argued that social learning was a neglected phenomenon in the social sciences because it did not arise from any "new information and analysis accomplished through PSI" (professional social inquiry).[93] They used the example of energy conservation that had little chance of being pursued until enough Americans *experienced* high fuel prices and lines at gasoline stations in the late 1970s. As Lindblom and Cohen put it: "The actual experience . . . leads to reconsidered positions rather than a professional investigator's examination of the existing circumstance or of feasible policies (that do not yet exist)." They went on to note that "the common opinion 'things will have to get worse before they get better' testifies to the possibility that a problem cannot be solved until people have had—or suffered—such experiences as will bring them to new attitudes and political dispositions."[94] And further, "various forms of social interaction. . . . substitute action for thought, understanding, or analysis."[95] The social learning experience itself becomes the source for initiating whatever conduct or action seems called for in addressing a problem. Even more critical is that such learning becomes collaborative to the extent that enough others experiencing a problem is a precondition for trying to do something about it—together.

Putting to one side social learning that comes from experiencing a problem, there have also been more positive grounds for social learning. When the historian Lawrence Cremin examined community sources of education throughout American history, it was in the *doing* that young people learned; experience that went beyond teachers, lessons, and books. Apprenticeship, which flourished, was an example of a pedagogy that combined "direct example" and "immediate participation." Social learning "went on anywhere and everywhere . . . in kitchens, manses, churches, meetinghouses, sheds erected in fields, and shops erected in towns; that pupils were taught by anyone and everyone . . . by parents, tutors, clergy-men, lay readers . . . physicians, lawyers, artisans and shopkeepers." Such social learning certainly did not originate in a classroom. In fact, Noah Webster's 1828 dictionary did not even mention schooling in the defini-tion of "educate."[96] Community sources contributed to the social learning of young people and most everyone else at one time or another. That is why Cremin took note that *experience*, "carefully observed and thought-fully considered" was a rich educative source. In the developing story of American education, Cremin, unlike many others, saw schools and col-leges, albeit increasingly central and vital, as just one learning source. Social learning amounted to what Thomas Jefferson thought of as "found education . . . one happens upon in the course of living a varied and reflec-tive life."[97] Cremin, more than any other historian of American education, recognized the long-standing importance of those who educated others—in churches, synagogues, libraries, museums, summer camps, benevolent societies, agricultural fairs, settlement houses, factories—all the formative influences of "mutual education" in public life where Americans learned from one another.

Throughout his work, Cremin argued that the variety of educational institutions and educators in America's far-flung communities, what he called "the ecology of education," has been a rich and enduring source beyond the school zone. I told him on one occasion that, given his the-ory of education, "we are all potential educators," but only "potential" educators because Cremin distinguished those who "purposefully" seek to change "others' thinking, behavior, or sensibilities" from those whose influence is not intentional. Nonetheless, there are still many potential educators whose curricula and classrooms lie beyond the school zone. There are ministers, priests, rabbis, librarians, curators, grant-makers, local history buffs, public television and print journalists, pro bono law-yers and paralegals, public health and day care staff, business trainers and employers, peer and youth group counselors, adult literacy and workshop instructors, self-help and community organizers, and all manner of vol-untary associations, their leaders and their websites. "Community educa-tors" have many different agendas—public safety, public health, the arts, environmental protection, job training, and on and on, but they can also be "purposeful" in nurturing the development of others' democratic skills while engaged with them in pursuing their varied agenda. Such social learning can be the subtext of almost any community organization or initiative. David Mathews of the Kettering Foundation recently described how the parochial, prosaic offerings of the so-called undereducated can have value beyond their knowing: "People's first reaction was 'I never taught anybody anything,' perhaps because they associated teaching with classrooms. Later, however, they described numerous ways in which they had, in fact, educated others. They had taught basic skills like cooking, sewing, and taking care of equipment. Their 'lessons' included the virtues of patience, persistence and sacrifice."[98] Social learning from experience requires no credentials on anyone's part.

The Ice Cream Factory (II)

While writing this book I learned that young Dewey from Chapter 1 had left the Ice Cream Factory. It was puzzling—why did he go? I wanted to know so I caught up with him wandering the streets of the old town he knew so well.

Brown: Tell me, Dewey, why are you here and not making Butter Almond back in Building #75?

Dewey: Oh, I guess it goes back to the personnel officer, Mr. Dasher, telling me that I didn't learn anything from my mother about making ice cream that would help me in the Factory.

Brown: Well, did you learn anything from your mother?

Dewey: Of course, but the Ice Cream Factory and my immediate superior, "Big Boy" at Butter Almond, pursued a very different formula. At the Factory they're interested in volume, not weight.

Brown: I'm not sure what you mean . . .

Dewey: Well, you have to understand that the Factory measures its ice cream by volume, not weight, so they add a lot of air to the products they produce—including Butter Almond.

Brown: They add air?

Dewey: Sure, they save money by selling more air than ice cream. Look, ice cream, however it's made, is a whipped product with some nourishment but a lot of air. My mother's homemade ice cream was hand-churned and very dense. No wonder Mr. Dasher told me to "forget about my mother's ice cream," but what he didn't tell me was about the air they add at the Ice Cream Factory. Air makes the ice cream easier to scoop—just look at how popular their product is. Everyone accepts it as made, air and all, and the Factory has made a fantastic business out of it.

Brown: Do you think the public knows that a lot of what the Factory makes is more air than ice cream?

Dewey: I doubt it, but why should they care?

Brown: Well, you must have cared or you wouldn't have left.

Dewey: I guess.

Brown: Tell me, Dewey, did you ever find any of the green glass windows?

Dewey: Are you kidding? No one I found ever looks for the windows, and even if they did they wouldn't find any they could look out from. It's a very closed shop.

Brown: But why did you leave then for the old town that you thought had no future?

Dewey: I'm not so sure of that anymore. I got to thinking if I could find enough others to compete with the Ice Cream Factory, or even better to somehow take over that place and make it . . . (Dewey paused).

Brown: Make it what?

Dewey: Make it more accessible for those in the old town, make its ice cream with less air . . .

Brown: That would be quite an undertaking on your part, Dewey.

Dewey: Oh, it would take enough others besides me. Some of them might be right there in the Ice Cream Factory. I think of Mr. Dasher, who has long been tired of his job. Perhaps he lost interest after leaving Lime Sherbert where he made his name. There must be others like him.

Brown: Do you really think there are enough others at the Factory or in the old town who can make a difference?

Dewey: I don't know. Anyway, I'd start with the windows, the ones that don't look out. I'd put in real ones you could see through so those on the outside and those in the inside could get a better look at each other.

Brown: You told me about less air in the ice cream. What about fewer flavors?

Dewey: Oh, I think there will always be new flavors coming along. It's not the number of them, but whether each has something to offer.

Brown: Mr. Dasher insists that all flavors in the Factory are equally good, and you agreed since it was a rule for working there.

Dewey: Oh, I should have thought a little more about that. A rule like that certainly keeps everybody tending to their own special flavor, but now I think it was just a way of making sure that no one would change anything in the Factory, including all the flavors, each with its own Society.

Brown: And don't the Factory's marketing people take care that each flavor gets its due?

Dewey: Oh sure, but I think that each flavor, whatever it is, should really have something to offer.

Brown: Well, maybe, as you say, if enough others in the Factory and old town get together, they could focus on the flavors worth making.

Dewey: Who knows . . .?

Brown: By the way, your name is Dewey—did you ever hear of John Dewey?

Dewey: Did he invent the Dewey decimal system?

Brown: No, that was Melvil Dewey. You know, John Dewey would heartily approve of your leaving the Ice Cream Factory and entertaining the possibility of reorganizing it in some way.

Dewey: Why, was he an ice cream expert?

Brown: No, more like a philosopher about ice cream and many other things. Dewey was one of the first to point the finger at the Factory and suggest there were better ways to make ice cream.

Dewey: Sounds interesting. Did he write books, too?

Brown: Oh, sure, many of them. Well, what comes next, Dewey?

Dewey: I wish I knew. But there's got to be more than the Ice Cream Factory. The old town is withering and the Factory offers too much false hope.

With that Dewey and I shook hands, and he headed off into the great unknown.

CHAPTER 5

Everybody Counts

In a letter to James Madison in 1789, Thomas Jefferson asserted: "The earth should belong . . . always to the living generation." For the rest of Jefferson's life, he "often returned to the linked themes of freedom, fresh starts, and the folly of old customs and laws binding new generations."[1] America did not start out as a democracy. It took several generations to evolve. And just as the elitism of conservative Whigs and Federalists gradually yielded to Jeffersonians and Jacksonians,[2] the credentialed experts of our time may find it advisable to make more room for, and work with, engaged citizens. Perhaps the "living generation" of this era might look anew at the culture of professionalism that has largely ignored the experience and judgment of ordinary citizens for more than a century. In creating such an unnecessary divide, many experts assume they can serve the public interest on *their* terms, and too many citizens have come to accept the terms. Too many professionals may work for the public, but not with the public. It is the "task monopoly" of credentialed specialists that "shrinks the space of democratic authority and disables and immobilizes citizens who might occupy that space."[3] As William Schambra put it: When professionals already "have a map of the problem in their heads and a map of the solution . . . no matter how open-ended they say they are to community input, that's all it is, is community input."[4] John McKnight has gone even further to argue that there are many professionals in the service industry "who believe that they are in direct competition with communities for the power to correctly define problems [and] provide scientific solutions.[5]

Matt Leighninger has described the "ongoing professionalization of the civic field" with some irony, and feels that despite "efforts to move beyond expert rule, local leaders are seeking more experts."[6] When I interviewed Leighninger in 2009, he was concerned that "the day-to-day work of solving public problems is centered on the needs and interests of professionals," when instead "what works best for democratic governance is to go where the citizens are and center the discussions around their needs and interests." Leighninger's continuing concern about the professionalization of the civic field does not foreclose the possibility that what he says can be learned from "committed amateurs without formal training."[7] According to Leighninger, "democratic civic engagement" works best when "(1) assembling a diverse group of citizens; (2) combining small groups and large forum opportunities both face-to-face and online; (3) offering a range of options, arguments and information to those participating; and (4) aiming to produce "tangible actions and outcomes."[8]

There has been much written about deliberative theory, and deliberation has been practiced in many venues. Derek Barker and his colleagues at the Kettering Foundation noted that "due largely to the influence of [Jurgen] Habermas and [John] Rawls, the dominant conception of deliberation that emerged in political theory in the 1980s and 1990s was the ideal of rational discourse governed by the norms of reciprocity, inclusion and (in some versions) the search for consensus."[9] How has the social scaffolding of deliberation been put to use? I should start with my friend and colleague, David Mathews, president of the Kettering Foundation, who, along with a talented staff and a worldwide range of "associates," has provided the research and rationale of deliberative practices that make room for both reason *and* judgment. The Kettering Foundation has worked with the National Issues Forums (NIF) for many years, exploring how deliberative town meetings can build "greater local capacity for shared decision-making on contentious issues."[10] Kettering research has prepared deliberative guides for NIFs, "nonpartisan, nationwide network whose participants include an array of civic educational and professional groups, organizations, and individuals that promote public deliberation in communities across the country. . . . Each year major issues of concern are identified by the NIF network. Issue guides are prepared to provide an overview of the problem and alternative approaches to dealing with it and to help those attending the forums frame the deliberation."[11]

Potluck Deliberation

My argument, in part, is that America's culture of professionalism has "undermined the self-confidence of many Americans to look after problems within their reach or to collaborate with professionals who often seem beyond their reach." Too many experts in think tanks, government agencies, and academe assume that they can solve all manner of public problems while ignoring or excluding citizen participation. In Chapter 2 I offered the provocation that experts are no less ignorant about most things than average citizens. So it is entirely possible that citizens and experts could, on equal terms, find common ground where everyone has something to contribute and something to learn—a kind of "potluck deliberation"—about problems of health care, education, poverty, family decline, racism, drug abuse, illegal immigration, scarcity of water resources, abuse of the environment, and on and on. What if public space could be established and shared by credentialed specialists and citizens who could look to each other for help? It would be territory that belonged to no one in particular, a kind of no-man's land, where experts and citizens could meet to exchange their respective gifts. It would be a space that could provide a way to speculate and share rather than merely confirm what is already known and accepted. It would be a way to discover together a potential that democracy makes possible but does not guarantee.[12]

There is the possibility that potluck deliberation that involved experts and citizens would put everyone on equal footing. Neither experts nor citizens alone have the wherewithal to resolve most public problems, much less "solve" them. They may not be equal in their respective capacities, but, as John Dewey noted, "equality denotes an effective regard for whatever is distinctive and unique in each."[13] Experts using abstract reasoning and citizens exercising judgment from personal experience need each other when addressing public problems. It is similar to James Scott's useful analogy of combining the talents of sea captains navigating their ships across vast oceans with the "local knowledge" of harbormasters who are needed to bring such ships to dock. "Navigation on the open sea (a more 'abstract' space)" is vastly different from "piloting a ship through traffic in a particular port." The latter is "a highly contextual skill."[14] So, too, the knowledge of experts applied to more abstract spaces needs the "local knowledge" of citizens acquired from experience in their parochial settings. It is very unlikely that experts will be as familiar with the specific "harbors" and "ports" that citizens know well and know better.[15] "Local knowledge" challenges and breaks apart the generalized certainties that experts have come to rely on when lacking the experience of citizen-harbormasters. The "social learning" from experience, discussed in Chapter 4, is one dimension of what citizens can bring to any potluck deliberation.

Bernie Ronan, a former public administrator, put it this way: "It's not to say that people are latently expert, only that they have a lot more learning in their heads than they are given credit for."[16] Ronan acknowledged that experts also bring their own kind of social learning acquired from experience—"a kind of core knowledge that a practitioner builds up over years of work."[17] The personal skills and judgment of experts acquired from such experience is the kind of tacit knowledge that complements, rather than competes with, the local knowledge that citizens bring. Esoteric knowledge can be obscure and intimidating, but the tacit knowledge of credentialed specialists combined with the local knowledge of citizens makes the combination more accessible and productive. Donald Schon sees such common ground as "reflection in action"—that is, learning by doing and thinking about it in retrospect. According to Schon, professionals can help citizens be reflective, since professionals may do more of that in practice than citizens do in everyday life.[18] Schon, however, cautions that the professional practitioner can overlearn what he knows and "afflict his clients with the consequences of his narrowness and rigidity."[19] For Schon, the reflective practitioner would say "I am presumed to know, but I cannot be the only one in the situation to have relevant and important knowledge. My uncertainties may be a source of learning for me and for them."[20] For example, after a decade of experience in the political life of New York City and State, I was admitted through a side door at Yale's School of Management, not to teach political science, but instead to use my experience to create new teaching cases. I knew that students could not adequately learn about politics by reading a how-to manual. My classroom cases were no substitute for learning on the job, but they did help students better understand what they might expect in the "real world," instead of fashioning campaign signs that say: "It's People, not Politics." On the contrary, the idea is that "politics" *is* people.

Without opportunities for potluck deliberation, experts are not likely to get enough feedback from citizens to improve their own performance. And that is why citizens and professionals could both profit from working together as equals. The problem remains, however, that the habits developed by experts and would-be professionals in academe can make it much harder to foster a rough equality with citizens, which, in time, can encourage such feedback. For example, the Extension Service of land-grant universities was established in the mid-nineteenth century to share academic research with those whose labor was centered on what their farms could produce and bring to market. Unfortunately, there has been a long-standing divide between specialists in academe and those in various agricultural pursuits. Often, the specialists think they know better and those on the ground believe their expertise is ignored.

As discussed in Chapter 2, expertise and ignorance are inextricably joined in any credentialed specialist. Acknowledging their own limitations, without surrendering their sovereignty within specialized limits, would allow experts to accept a rough equality with citizens. It would not be a patronizing gesture, but an acknowledgment that the potential for finding solutions lies somewhere between them. John Dewey argued: "academic expertise in a democratic society . . . must be tested in the public world as well as disciplinary communities."[21] Tom Bender thinks that modern service professions did not become "socially irresponsible, but their contributions to society began to follow from their self-definitions rather than from a reciprocal engagement with general public discourse."[22] Philosopher Elizabeth Minnich told me:

> Narrow notions of rationality that are akin to those of scientific rationality in pressing toward certainty, and so also predictability, are dangerous to democracy. Certainty and predictability before which dissent is error and refusal to behave as predicted is at best anomalous do not seem to me qualities we ought to want in a would-be democracy . . . You may have to think with all sorts of people in order to put your own thoughts into shape . . . This is wise politically; it also recalls Kant's maxims of common human understanding: think consistently, think coherently, and think from the position of others. A whole different sort of authority is sometimes granted to those who do that well.[23]

Potluck deliberation might require some forbearance on the part of experts and some nerve on the part of citizens. Citizens would have to be willing to ask what some might consider stupid questions, such as "What do you do, and how do you do it?"[24] But questions are not stupid when they offer an opportunity to learn. I have written elsewhere: "When experts have to explain themselves to others in simple terms, it forces them to put aside the private shorthand and vocabulary used by insiders and to find bridging language that connects with those who are on the outside looking in. . . . Too often there is overreaching by experts or mindless delegation of authority to them when non-experts don't take the time to learn what someone's expertise really consists of and what it doesn't."[25] Professor Stuart Firestein offers a more constructive question: "Ask them what they're trying to find out . . . emphazing ignorance makes everyone feel equal . . . dumb and ignorant are not the same."[26] What is likely to happen in potluck deliberation, whether those participating acknowledge it or not, is that citizens may feel *vulnerable* when asking questions, and experts may feel vulnerable when not taking cover behind esoteric language or staying within their respective niches. However, one of the by-products of engaging with citizens on equal terms would be acknowledging that everyone's ignorance about most things is unavoidable. Firestein argues: "Knowledge is a big subject. Ignorance is bigger. And it is more interesting . . . questions are more relevant than answers. Questions are bigger than answers . . . Forget the answers, work on the questions."[27] If credentialed specialists can acknowledge their ignorance *and* that they have something to learn from citizens, it removes some of the pretension and mystery of what is known and what is yet to be learned. This could also be a valuable lesson for citizens who have been raised on media to think that someone, somewhere in expert circles just might have the answers for most everything that ails them. It might lead to their fresh questioning of what is already "known"—not to denigrate what experts may offer, but to practice a healthy skepticism that requires experts to reconsider perhaps what they have come to take for granted.[28]

Some credentialed specialists for the best of reasons might disqualify themselves from "potluck deliberation" when as advocates, as well as experts, they take up a singular cause. On the other hand, nothing keeps them from contributing to citizen understanding of complicated issues, if the objective of such advocate-experts is not just a matter of winning or losing, but also aiding the learning process of those whose understanding and support they seek. The adversarial culture, promoted by the media and practiced by politicians, would be counterproductive for experts and citizens in potluck deliberation, both of whom could learn more by suspending, at least temporarily, the intransigence of their findings or opinions. It is quite possible that experts in a no-man's land beyond peer oversight and citizens without a fixed agenda could let down their guard.

This approach might foster new appetites for what others bring to the table.

Potluck deliberation might also encourage experts to reconsider staying within the narrow boundaries of their credentialed specialization and denying whatever personal gifts they might have to offer. I have written elsewhere: "An obvious but neglected fact is that those who are talented enough to be experts are also talented enough to help in other ways. Does the pursuit of expertise claim all the other talents they had before they became experts?"[29] Potluck deliberation might lead experts to engage all of their talents, not just their expertise. If so, credentialed specialists might more readily accept being part of a community of interest rather than just being a member of a particular profession. Tom Bender wisely notes a locality "offers to the academic the particularity, the concreteness, of lived experience in time and place."[30]

A potluck deliberation might begin with everyone sitting in a circle to help establish the equality of those in attendance, much like the teachers and students around the Harkness Table (see Chapter 4). When I asked Joni Doherty, director of the New England Center for Civic Life at Franklin Pierce University, why she formed circles when pursuing deliberative dialogue, she responded:

> We always form circles during our forums, both on and off campus. During the few times we have not, or even when someone chooses to sit outside the circle, in a second outer ring, it always affects the tone of the discussion. Typically the forum becomes less conversational and more a series of statements about individual positions. Those who are not 'face to face' also tend to offer comments that are more contentious or provocative, or to sit silently and listen. The circle by its nature limits the number of participants. This, in turn, insures that the number will be small enough . . . for participants to fully engage in the dialogic interaction necessary for authentic deliberation.[31]

There are, however, many potential problems in undertaking potluck deliberation between experts and citizens. Consider the problem of reaching out to the like-minded who tend to self-segregate on media and online sites that champion and reinforce their already predisposed opinions. Recently, a reporter for the *New York Times* saw such self-segregation in America as both a cause and an effect of the current political paralysis inside the Beltway. "All this adds up to a kind of political echo chamber, in which like-minded thinking reinforces one another."[32] What the like-minded are sure to bring are their passions for how certain problems should be solved or at least mitigated. One such "passion" is a consequence of what Michael Sandel calls "the era of market trium-phalism" coinciding "with a time when public discourse has been largely empty of moral and spiritual substance." Sandel thinks that "our only hope of keeping markets in their place is to deliberate openly and publicly about the meaning of the goods and social practices we prize.[33] Sandel, however, unintentionally slights the moral and spiritual passions of many citizens that still dictate what counts for them in discussing current issues and problems. Certainly, there is no guarantee that a potluck deliberation could not go off the rails. Still, it would be interesting to see how "passions" might serve rather than detract from the daunting task of finding common ground. Not everyone in a potluck deliberation will be dispassionate, but if there were a range of opinions and attitudes, the deliberation might get the passionate and dispassionate to listen and learn from each other.

Chapter 4 acknowledged the importance of *diversity* in treating knowledge as a social construct. Such diversity is often neglected or even resented by those who have already made up their minds about the issues and problems that confront them. But like a good classroom or community forum, a potluck deliberation could offer information and insights not previously considered by those who came predisposed in their opinions. This is why the presence of experts could be important, not to dominate or dictate the course of the deliberation, but to provide new perspectives. Their expertise would not be played as a trump card but rather as a wild card that others might use to enrich their understanding of whatever issue or problem was front and center. I used to tell students: "It is not enough to think you know what the problem is. It also matters what each of those in your group think the problem is. It is not enough to think you know what the solution is. It also matters if the others think that your solution fits their own conceptions of what the problem is. And even if your solution does, it is possible that they may think they have better solutions than yours."[34]

If those participating in a potluck deliberation came out a different door from the one they entered, such learning could be an end in itself. While they may not have found all the answers, the deliberation provides a valuable experience that could lead to fresh perspectives. Differences that emerged in potluck deliberation, whether over markets, morals, or whatever, could also help participants learn about what politics is really about—an often despised beast but a necessary one in any exchange about things that really matter. Passionate citizens have every right to resent condescending attitudes of those who supposedly know more, know better. I have already noted that when experts focus on the substance of an issue without considering the politics, it is often a vain attempt to eliminate the unmanageable number of variables that politics requires. A potluck deliberation would likely be a difficult experience for those with a professional mind-set or for those whose ideology brooks no compromise. Elizabeth Minnich provided some perspective: "Many faculty see as their contribution to democracy, i.e. training [students] in 'rational analysis and decision-making' . . . [but] it can turn [them] against real political engagement simply because it is rare indeed that public hearings, debates, marches, rallies, strategizing are characterized by disinterested, logical analysis of data and/or well-cast abstract principles. . . . So the educated can find themselves repelled as well as disempowered in real political life, having not practiced the arts of listening . . . empathy, sympathy, imagination, rhetoric, compromise."[35]

Certainly, experts in any potluck deliberation should not dominate with dispassionate analyses, nor should they necessarily defer to the expressed interests of citizens sitting around the same table who are at some emotional distance from such credentialed "objectivity." What then could be done to help equalize the relationship between experts and citizens? Experts might concede that unused citizen capacities would be needed for follow-through actions. It would be the difference between *explanation*, which experts could provide, and *response*, which would be more citizen doing. Knowledge-based explanations and proposals would get a potluck deliberation halfway across the pond—people-based responses would be needed to get to the other side. Finding a reason to participate *beyond* a potluck deliberation would not just be a matter of exhortation by those who attempted to assemble or to organize a follow-through. It is more likely that those who participated might find that the deliberative experience itself drew them in and led them on. It is much the same when examining how a social convention takes hold—a circumstance prompts a coordinating "solution" and enough others join in to make it work. And important by-products of the deliberative experience could lead some participants to "discover in themselves . . . new democratic potentials."[36] Sara Evans and Harry Boyte have argued that such discovery includes people learning "to speak in public, run meetings, analyze problems and their sources, write leaflets and so forth—the sort of skills that are essential to sustaining democracy."[37]

However, the range and duration of citizen involvement are never easy to predict. "How far?" "How long?" are questions that have no answers except as citizens sort them out with those confronting the same questions. Consider some of the reasons and excuses that may be offered. Elsewhere I have written: "I think of our preference to be free of social problems, which our mobility accommodates, as a preference for 'exit.' The problem doesn't go away, but we do. I think of our preference to have government solve our problems for us as a preference for 'delegation.' We have better things to do. I think of our preference to put individual interest ahead of social interest as a preference for 'private gain'—one of the 'better things' to do. And I think of our preference not to be put at a personal disadvantage as a preference for 'parity' . . . the expectation that others will do their part."[38]

Potluck deliberation would be just a beginning. Problem solving would necessarily become more social-driven than cognitive-driven, leading to less predictable action and with the likelihood of different priorities than the deliberation itself. Problem solving with experts in the lead can too often be knowledge-based, a static hold-still habit, rather than people-based, which is nonlinear and dynamic—a continuum of improvised actions and revisions. "Wicked problems," which may involve moral and intellectual disagreement, usually require the attention of citizens over an extended period of time. Those engaged might remain uncertain about their choices as various courses of action are considered and pursued—something like the trial and error that a medical doctor undertakes, making a tentative diagnosis and prescribing treatment interventions to see what works and doesn't. The doctor wants more information, more feedback, more time. Prescription quantities are limited, dosages are adjusted, side effects are observed. Of course, many of those participating in a potluck deliberation may already be linked to agencies, organizations, or committees with resources available for following through on whatever emerges. Harry Boyte has perceptively noted that "structures and institutions are neither the solution to complex public problems nor our enemies, but rather the tools."[39] There might even be new associations, formal or informal, that emerge from this type of deliberation. Whether temporary or more lasting, such associations might be used like play dough, a modeling compound of young children, when there was some resolution worth pursuing.[40]

The Precedent of American Juries

Some might say that there is little precedent for putting experts and citizens on equal terms, but they would be wrong. Juries sitting as equals with judges and counsel is a long-standing practice in America's legal history. "Jurors literally co-create justice with court professionals by testing evidence, legal theories, and ultimately the law of the land against everyday knowledge, practical experience, and wide-ranging moral awareness." This was the response of Albert Dzur to a question of mine in an interview I conducted to learn more about his work concerning "democratic professionalism."[41] Political theorist Lynn Sanders has also noted: "When jury deliberations are focused more on eliciting a range of views instead of on the common problem of arriving at a verdict, they appear likely to provoke both a more considerate discussion and one that leaves jurors more satisfied with their participation."[42]

Some might dispute the competence of juries as compared to the experienced competence of a presiding judge, but one observer of the jury system found that "almost always the collective memory of the jury is superior to the individual memory of the most highly qualified judge." And an "amateur assembly is more likely to bring desired diverse experience to the evidence than would a collection of professional judges."[43] Potluck deliberation would not be for testing the memory of citizens as compared to the memory of an expert, but a diverse group of citizens would be as likely to bring collective "local knowledge" as valuable to such an exchange as the tacit knowledge of an expert. The exercise of citizen judgment and the assertion of expert intellect would be complementary.

When people ask me, "Just what is this potluck deliberation you're talking about?" I find myself citing jury deliberation as an example. Nancy Thomas and Peter Levine indicate that "a *public deliberation* operates in much the same way [as the judicial process and the role of juries]: people come together to study a social or political issue, give careful consideration to the facts, identify possible solutions, weigh the pros and cons of each choice, and then make a decision as to how the issue should be addressed."[44] The jury experience differs from potluck deliberation in that the former relies on the legal expertise of judges and counsel and the latter assumes no strict division of roles as exist in a courtroom trial. Still, the deliberation that jurors share in seeking to come to a verdict often involves asking for clarification from the courtroom experts available to them. The jury experience confirms that reaching any judgment requires collaboration among court personnel and jury members. Like jury service, those who come together in a potluck deliberation would be interested in the deliberative *process*—a process that should be fair and thorough with experts learning from citizens and citizens learning from experts. Unlike a courtroom trial or a National Issues Forum, there might be no conclusive moment in the process. However, the diversity of the participants and the rough equality among them, would be a valuable learning experience for experts finding their "peers" among those participating rather than the usual credentialed specialists they normally consult.

Potluck deliberation certainly would not have the legal or constitutional standing of a jury. Without public authority, those engaged in such "deliberation" could not expect whatever emerged from the process to have anything but a persuasive effect on public opinion or the responses of established organizations and government agencies. Although participating in a potluck deliberation would not give citizens the same standing as serving on a jury, the comparison is meant to underscore the standing that ordinary citizens deserve when sharing with experts responsibility for solving social problems. The very experience of deliberating as equals could influence how they might find ways of continuing to work together with perhaps significant ripple effects in academe, professional practice, and community organizing. "The jury is not just a fixture of a steady administration of justice, but must be understood as part of a heritage of internal arrangements that preserve amateurism."[45] Potluck deliberation would be a reassertion of "amateurs" and an attempt to reassess the culture of professionalism that too often separates experts from citizens, rather than bringing them together.

Academe's Deliberative Role

What more can be done in academe to prepare would-be professionals for the important but often neglected citizen role? It is entirely possible that students, whether would-be professionals or not, could acquire a new standing in their classrooms if more attention were paid to what citizenship involves as much as what credentials confer. John Saltmarsh and Mathew Hartley skeptically asked: "To what extent do current courses allow students to develop their own opinions about various issues and then learn and practice the precepts of public deliberation to refine them?" And so they urge greater classroom standing for students: "Faculty should enact pedagogical practices that reflect active and collaborative forms of teaching and learning and that draw upon and value the knowledge and experience that all students bring to the classroom as assets in the education process."[46] Such practices would do much to avoid Gerald Graff's criticism that there is "something unhealthy about teachers who mindlessly preach to the converted, never having to encounter an opposing view from anyone of equal authority."[47]

Class experience is an important introduction to what would-be professionals can eventually do both as professionals and citizens if more attention is paid to *how* they learn, not just *what* they learn. Saltmarsh and Hartley think "this means that faculty should not only frame disciplinary contents in terms of the public dimension of the discipline, but also provide opportunities for students to practice the skills of democracy through the course."[48] On the other hand, one faculty member I queried thought that students at the undergraduate level may have too much of the upper hand these days. "I think students actually have more power than they ever had in classrooms before. Many professors feel bullied by student pressure and other forces into assigning fewer readings, providing less critique. And grade inflation. On many campuses faculty are not allowed to require students to attend or participate in class, assign textbooks, or convene their class without an elms site. This suggests much power to scaffold a genuine learning environment has been taken away from professors, and handed over to consumer interests and satisfaction polls—and I don't think that is good for education."[49] At the graduate level, however, Elizabeth Minnich notes, "What seems key to me is that students be invited into a discussion in ways that engage their own memories, experiences, values, assumptions with those of theorists, empiricists, practitioners. . . . Judgment cannot be taught directly, but it can be practiced using examples, and . . . the examples can come from anywhere but are most effective when they emerge from the students' own lives and concerns." Minnich went on to say that without such classroom practice, "How many . . . are still able to do what they really love, to change enough, to engage with differing publics and issues, when they've behaved themselves throughout graduate school, and then seven long years [to get tenure]?[50]

Parker Palmer put succinctly what he thinks all students, undergraduate or graduate, must learn: "Democracy . . . is not something we *have* but something we must *do*."[51] Something students *do* is certainly at the heart of civic efforts that many are currently undertaking in nearby communities with which they are "engaged." And "civic" or "community engagement" also includes a growing number of faculty members. Nonetheless, it remains unclear whether such interest and efforts are doing much to change the antidemocratic hierarchies and practices in academe. Saltmarsh and Hartley conclude: "Rather than openly questioning the prevailing norms, customs and structures of the academy, civic engagement efforts have instead adapted in order to ensure their acceptance and legitimacy within it."[52] Dan Butin speaks for many others when he notes: "the current model of community engagement is premised on and driven by the overarching leitmotif of the transformation of higher education," but agrees with Saltmarsh that it is a "stalled" movement.[53] Butin would have "community engagement . . . become an intellectual movement" embracing "the scholarship of engagement. . . . [W]hat we do with, for, and in the community must be open to the same type of scrutiny as any other legitimate academic practice."[54] However, would such an academic emphasis leave the culture of professionalism relatively unaffected?

Taking a different route, Martin Carcasson, a faculty member at Colorado State University, is teaming his Center for Public Deliberation (CPD) with the citizens of Ft. Collins, Colorado, and giving undergraduate students a major role in fostering deliberative practices. Carcasson has observed that "community members are consistently amazed by the fact that not only are students at a public meeting, but they seem to be running it."[55] Carcasson offered an interesting distinction for students working with him at the CPD: "I try to explain to students that this isn't a typical class, or a typical profession[al]-student relationship. The CPD is an 'organization' and they are part of such an organization."[56] His distinction, intentional or not, puts students on a more equal footing with him. I asked Carcasson if he would further clarify his ongoing work:

> **Brown:** Your work addresses the need for developing community capacity, especially for wicked problems, which you argue go beyond the reach of activists and experts. In founding the CSU Center for Public Deliberation,

with an impartial, process-focused role in Ft. Collins, why have students, whom you have named student associates . . . proven to be a perfect fit for such an undertaking?

Carcasson: I believe democracy needs smart, passionate people focused on improving the quality of our public discourse for democracy to work as it should. The problem is such people are in very short supply. Most smart, passionate people are already engaged in issues and have taken positions. They can't walk into a room and be the impartial facilitator because they took a stand at city council the week before, or people simply know their position already. Such people are also already very busy, therefore unlikely to have the time to dedicate to support deliberative practice. Students, on the other hand, are unknown, and with many city issues, may not have a strong position internally yet either. And when you have the ability to have an application process and be able to choose high quality students, and then provide them class credit to account for their time, you have developed a critical community resource. I now have a group of around thirty trained students available each semester to help run a wide variety of community events.

Brown: You have noted that deliberative democracy has moved beyond a purely rational discourse era and as practiced now rarely seeks consensus. Does that make it less a problem-solving practice and more a process-centered form of inclusion of those in a community?

Carcasson: I believe it needs to do both . . . Once you have lots of voices in the room . . . then you need processes that help people work through the groan zone, and do the difficult work of developing understanding of each other and addressing the inherent tensions to democratic decision-making. Finally, we can't simply talk forever, so at some point we need to move on to convergent thinking, and work at making decisions and supporting specific actions. . . . The reason I rarely seek consensus is because addressing wicked problems will not lead to consensus, because there is not one best answer to uncover. Consensus is perhaps still the idealistic goal to seek, but my concern is that pushing for consensus likely closes off voices and process too much. Therefore the work we do likely has several decision points along the way, with some of those decisions being individuals or groups making decisions to act in various ways, or perhaps an institutional body making a policy decision. For example, when projects are tied to providing a better sense of the public voice to decision makers, we don't seek consensus in our process, we seek to improve and refine the public voice through the process, and then accurately report to the decision makers what people think once they have been exposed to high quality deliberation.

Brown: Does the role of experts in deliberative inquiry essentially remain to the side or apart from engaged publics? From your vantage point, do such experts stay within the self-imposed limits of their expertise or do they explore individual gifts that go beyond such limits?

Carcasson: We are working on developing a clearer sense of the ways in which experts help and hinder deliberative processes, with a particular eye for how to manage expert contributions before, during, and after a process. Overall, we feel they must play a role, and likely more of a role than Kettering/NIF tends to assign them. But identifying how to take advantage of what they can add, without suffering unduly from what problems they can cause, can be a difficult process.[57]

Carcasson's efforts at CSU are a work in progress and there are likely to be many variations of what experts, citizens, *and* students can do together, not only at CSU, but also across the broad expanse of academe. In a very different setting, it is worth looking at the work of Joni Doherty, director of the New England Center for Civic Life (NECCL) at Franklin Pierce University in Rindge, New Hampshire. The NECCL emerged in 1998 committed to democratic social change. When a festering controversy remained unresolved between the towns of Rindge and neighboring Jaffrey about where new schools would be located, NECCL was asked to help. Doherty introduced a deliberative dialogue process for local residents and also offered them meeting space at Franklin Pierce for a weekly dialogue. As time went on the dialogue of those participating found common ground in the Jaffrey-Rindge Cooperative School District.

Seeing a town/gown opportunity more than ten years ago, Doherty, along with her colleague, Douglas Challenger, a founder of NECCL, coordinated a three-year college-community collaboration using the practices of deliberative democracy to address issues concerning the future development of Rindge—appropriately named Rindge 2020: The Challenge of Growth. The participants addressed questions about what they wanted the town to be like in 2020, and learned that the practice of dialogue and deliberation was a way "to potentially overcome the pitfalls of interest group politics and adversarial forms of communication" that often discouraged people "from participating in community affairs," leaving the town "fractured and divided."[58] "Citizens realized that *they* had the answers to their own local problems and grew to trust the deliberative community as a way to access their own collective wisdom."[59] I recently asked Doherty what outcomes of the Rindge 2020 project have endured.

She told me "the most significant outcome was the commitment by the town to purchase land over a major aquifer." Before Rindge 2020, "this kind of purchase was perceived as preservation, something that should be done with private moneys. As a result of the forums, residents now saw it as a public resource, even though there isn't a public water or sewage system. Other outcomes include the creation of a full-time position for a town planner . . . the creation of an Economic Advisory Council . . . and the Rindge Connection, a newsletter jointly produced by the University and the town to fill the void of not having a local newspaper."[60]

The focus of NECCL gradually moved on to projects with faculty and students becoming more involved, as well as securing NECCL's place and funding within the university. Students convened and led forums that, according to Doherty, gave them a "sense of agency" and provided "other students with an opportunity to practice deliberation." And many of the students have found opportunities to take such deliberative practices and apply them in other activities.[61] Doherty added her insight that students acquire the *art of listening* in such practices, which "might help us all slow down and enjoy each other more" and "would certainly enrich our civic life too."[62]

Phronesis for the Asking (II)

"HOMELESS MAN STABS CITY VISITOR." That was the lead story on the 11 o'clock news. The next morning, the *Boot Valley Sentinel* carried the same stabbing headline and story: "Last night, a homeless man, known locally as Mr. V, stabbed Mary Lou Frank, 33, in the right shoulder as she was entering the gift shop at the Appleton Hotel. Police called to the scene could offer no motive for the attack. Ms. Frank was rushed to the Memorial Hospital where she remained overnight. A hospital spokesman told the *Sentinel* that Ms. Frank is in satisfactory condition and resting comfortably.

"Mr. V, whose real name is Carl Benjamin, no address, was taken by police to the Boot Valley State Hospital for Mental Disease for psychiatric observation. The stabbing occurred after Ms. Frank emerged from a tour bus at the Appleton where she is staying with a group of visitors from Bangor, Maine. The victim told police that she had never seen her assailant before and could give no reason for the assault.

"Police told reporters that for several months Mr. V 'made his home' on a grate outside the Appleton, which was apparently warmed by heat exhaust from the hotel's basement laundry room. Recently the Appleton management had put barbed wire over the grate. According to the hotel's doorman, John Klein, Mr. V had not been seen in the vicinity of the hotel for more than a month. Benjamin apparently acquired the name Mr. V from his habit of frequently thrusting both arms in the air and giving the victory sign to whomever he encountered on the streets of Boot Valley. Klein told the *Sentinel*, 'Mr. V's voice is very deep and resonant. When he gets agitated, it is like the old Walter Cronkite I remember going berserk.'

"A spokesman for the Boot Valley State Hospital said that Benjamin has a long history of mental illness but was never considered dangerous. Boot Valley police confirmed that Benjamin has no previous criminal record. Several years ago, Benjamin was discharged from Boot Valley State under the State Mental Hygiene Law that prohibits anyone from being involuntarily hospitalized 'unless release is likely to result in serious harm to the patient or others.'

"Responding to the Appleton Hotel stabbing, Alex Sampas, a Boot Valley attorney and advocate for the homeless, said last night, 'How many incidents does it take before City Hall finally does something?' Sampas plans to meet with the mayor soon.

"The Frank stabbing is the latest in a series of incidents that have recently occurred in the National Historic Park area. The National Historic Park designation has used the lumber mill history of the city as a substantial tourist attraction. Four nineteenth-century mills were restored along with parts of the Pennacook Canal and other period buildings clustered downtown. A museum, canal boats, trolleys, and a repertory theater soon followed. Four hundred thousand tourists visited Boot Valley last year. The city also attracted a high-tech employer, Larcom Semiconductor, and its substantial payroll. Larcom proceeded to build a new corporate headquarters in Boot Valley and put up a national training center for its technical and sales people in conjunction with the Appleton Hotel chain, which then completed a 500-room complex located next to the training center.

* * *

Mayor Paul Connally, with the reflex of the politician, stood up and warmly greeted Lucy Wood and Marcus Dewitt. Lucy Wood was friendly and outgoing, just like the mayor. She had been the director of the Boot Valley Tourist Bureau for three years, and her booster spirit infected everyone she met. She sold the city twenty-four hours a day. Although she was not a city employee (the bureau was a creature of downtown business interests, hotels, restaurants, and the arts community), Connally worked closely with Wood and appreciated her hard work and enthusiasm for the city. Marcus Dewitt had caught the mayor's attention with several op-ed pieces in the *Sentinel* about how local governments and their planning departments are critical players when it comes to dealing with social problems.

"Paul," Wood began, "we really have to do something. We've done so much to refurbish the city's image, and now we face the prospect that all this publicity will give us a very bad name. If tourists stop coming here, well, you know how devastating that will be."

"Lucy, I don't understand you. The stabbing will get lots of play in Boot Valley, but our visitors don't follow the local news."

"Paul, I'm not talking about the *Sentinel* and Channel 10. I got a call this morning from the *Boston Globe*. They're planning to do a story about all this. Wait till all of New England reads about Mr. V and all the things that have been going on. You know, the menacing over at the Historic Park, those people urinating against buildings, stumbling around, shouting obscenities at tour buses. The tour operators have stories that will make us look like New York City. It could ruin our sesquicentennial celebration."

"Why the *Boston Globe*? Why now?" the Mayor asked.

"You remember Don McNally? The young guy who used to write for the *Sentinel*? Well, he's at the *Boston Globe* now, and he's probably trying to make a big splash with his editors. He always did have a lurid style of writing. Remember that whole series that he did on prostitution down by the river?"

"Don't remind me." The mayor slumped in his chair. "OK, we've got a bigger problem than I thought." Waiting for a response, he looked at Dewitt.

"Mr. Mayor, this may come as a surprise given my academic interest in central planning and those op-eds of mine in the *Sentinel* you may have read . . ."

"Yes, professor, I read them . . ."

"Well, Mr. Mayor, I'm still learning, and the more I learn about this town the more I think that your policy wonks and planners should sit down with a cross section of Boot Valley citizens—the homeless problem deserves as much."

"But look, professor, those citizens will expect me and my administration to do something about the Mr. V headlines."

"Don't be so sure, Mr. Mayor. Of course, you have the financial resources they don't, but they may have their own experience with the problem and their own ideas about what should be done.""Lucy," Connally smiled, "do you really think we can turn this around in a week?"

"Of course not," Wood was unfazed. "But you have to do something." She lingered on "*something*." "I think what the professor here suggests makes some sense. The Appleton manager told me this morning that there has to be more to this than just barbed wire and police sirens and crisis intervention teams. The city has done almost nothing."

This time Connally was less gentle with Wood. "Look, I don't accept the characterization of some twit at the Appleton Hotel that we have done nothing. Alex Sampas has been peddling that nonsense around town for months. We have the shelter at St. Clare's, and the Red Cross is thinking of coming in with one of their own."

Wood looked chagrined. The mayor was too important to her, and she backed off, nodding her head in agreement. But DeWitt picked up the argument. "Mr. Mayor, if the perception is that your administration hasn't done much or done enough about the homeless, then get your people and some of the professionals from

Boot Valley State Hospital to sit down with those who live with the homeless problem day in and day out. Maybe they can help too."

Connally looked at Wood. "What are we talking about in terms of homeless numbers?"

Wood appeared ready for the question. "According to my sources, I would estimate that we've got 750 out there. Twenty homeless families—we're taking care of them already. Then there are fifty more, singles, you know, over at St. Clare's. Maybe fifty more total taken in by other churches and synagogues. I figure we have 500 out on the street, and half of them are crazy, mentally ill. The police chief told me the other half have spent some time in jail, alcohol, drugs—you name it."

"We're going to do something, professor. And Lucy, don't worry. I don't want Don McNally writing this story without our help any more than you do. The Boot Valley professionals out at State Hospital haven't found the answer. My consultants sure don't seem to know what to do. Maybe, just maybe, we've got ideas and talent in this town we haven't yet tapped." With that, Wood and DeWiit were escorted to the door.

Connally's assistant, Lucille, looked up from her desk outside. "Do you want to talk to Cody Jackson, Mr. Mayor?" "Is he on the line?"

"No, his office called earlier when you were with the others."

"Yes, get him please." The intercom buzzed. The mayor picked up the phone. "Hello, Cody?"

"Just a minute, please," Jackson's assistant responded. There was a moment's pause. The mayor had to smile. It was something of a game between VIPs, or perhaps it was their assistants, as to who would come on the line first. Cody Jackson was CEO of Larcom Semiconductor, the largest employer in Boot Valley.

"Hello, Paul, sorry to keep you waiting."

"That's OK, Cody. What's up?"

"I told the head of our training center that I would call you. Being right across from the Appleton, he's developed a nervous tic about this homeless problem. I know you've got your hands full, Paul, but I said I would pass on his concern to you."

"Do you share his concern, Cody?"

"Well, of course, we all would like something done. This kind of thing scares the hell out of our employees, especially the women going home at night. And if it gets around, it doesn't help recruiting either. Our training center is an introduction to Larcom and Boot Valley. We don't need a Mr. V greeting the company's newcomers."

The Mayor laughed. "No, it's not the kind of welcome wagon I had in mind either."

Jackson ended the banter. "Well, you have the homeless to worry about. I'll let you go."

"Cody, what do you think of my people and interested citizens having a sit-down together . . ."

Jackson interrupted. "You've got to be kidding, Paul. You were elected to handle these problems."

The mayor bridled. "Then I guess my only alternative is to lease some of that empty floor space in your training center for the homeless."

Jackson hissed a good-natured obscenity and hung up.

There was a commotion in the hallway as the mayor looked out at the bright klieg lights set up in the rotunda. The media had gathered and were crowded around Alex Sampas. Sampas was six-foot-five and stood above the others. Connally cut the glare by shading his eyes and then could see four rather unkempt and forlorn-looking men and women standing next to Sampas. The mayor could only guess that Sampas had brought some of Boot Valley's homeless along for a spontaneous press conference. Connally turned to Lucille: "That kid is a genius with the media."

Lucille Bernard seemed uninterested. "Will you see him when he's through with them?"

Connally hesitated for a moment. "Sure, but go down the hall and catch him before he brings that troupe in. I want to see him alone and no stunts, or he'll cool his heels out there all afternoon. Remind him that I took a street tour with him last month and met his clients without any press around. That's the way to do it. I don't want to be on the six o'clock news tonight. He does." Looking down the hallway, Connally muttered, "He's got his coverage already. He doesn't need me."

Alex Sampas was a graduate of an Ivy League college and law school that seemed remote from Connally's experience in the state university system. Two years ago Sampas left a prestigious Boston law firm to return to his hometown. In Boston he had made a name for himself doing pro bono work with the homeless, and he brought his talents and agenda to Boot Valley for more of the same.

Sampas started to stir the pot by telling everyone who would listen to him that the Connally administration was making conditions "deliberately bad" for the homeless in the vain hope that they would just go away. The young lawyer was instrumental in opening a shelter for the homeless at St. Clare's church, an institution with a long history in Boot Valley.

Sampas arrived breathless in the mayor's office.

"Catch your breath, Alex." The mayor patted the sofa, motioning the young man to sit down. "How did it go out there?"

"Beautiful. The press loves that kind of stuff. It's great for the cause." Sampas put his richly tooled briefcase on his lap and slumped down in the sofa. "Lucy Wood doesn't have her facts right. Since when did she become a census taker? We've got a lot more than twenty homeless families. More like fifty. St. Clare's has seventy-five singles every night, not fifty. She's close on the 500 out there on the street, but half of them are not mentally ill—probably only about 25 percent. What you people can't seem to grasp is the difference between bizarre behavior brought on by fatigue and the paranoia of street living, and actual psychiatric disorder."

"Does that explain Mr. V last night?" the Mayor asked.

"No, Carl's a real case." Sampas stood up and started pacing. "It's damn hard to persuade that type to come off the street in the first place. They've been pushed around all their lives by simpleminded bureaucrats and a few overdosing psychiatrists. They don't trust anyone—not you, not me, no one."

Sampas got up and stood over the mayor with his arms crossed. "Shelters, your honor, wherever you put them, are only tokenism. What we need is permanent housing and adequate support services, medical, psychiatric, job counseling, education—it's a long list. For years you guys have been tearing down their housing to build whatever brings in a buck. I understand that, but you've got to make a place for them."

The mayor's face flushed. Now he stood up too. "Don't lecture me, Alex. You've never held elected office. You may be the Pied Piper from Boston, but you don't have a clue as to how the system works here."

The young lawyer stood his ground. "Oh, I know how the system works. You're running for re-election next year, and you're running scared."

Connally brushed by Sampas, stood at the window, and took a deep breath. "You know the way you could really help me, Alex? Go out there and tell your media friends that my people and a cross section of citizens are going to sit down together and see if we can learn from each other to get this problem off dead-center. The professor from up the hill suggested it."

Alex winced. "You mean some know-it-all actually suggested that?"

"Sure," Connally laughed. "Why not, we might all learn something, including you, Alex, including you."

Sampas shrugged. "OK, I'll say it's a start anyway. Maybe it'll unlock a few bank vaults on the way—including yours, Mr. Mayor."

CHAPTER 6

Nurturing Others' Capacities

When we think of professionals who serve the interests of their students, clients, patients, we often do not stop to think what this service entails. Chapter 3 looked at self-interested practices on the part of some lawyers, doctors, and financial advisers, who put their interest in profits before the interests of those they ostensibly serve. There is also a more subtle form of professional self-interest, rarely acknowledged, that prolongs the dependence of those "served." It occurs when little professional attention or thought is given to helping those served to develop their capacity for self-reliance. "Capacity" refers to the potential of what someone can offer or the potential of what collaboration with others may lead to—a "we" capacity, not just a "me" capacity—which credentialed specialists often fail to acknowledge and develop. Almost twenty years ago, John McKnight took aim at professional services: "The social policy mapmakers . . . build a world based upon the emptiness of each of us—a model based upon deficiency and need. Communities depend upon capacities. Systems commodify deficiencies."[1] More recently, McKnight with Peter Block went on to say: "Professionalization is the market replacement for a community that has lost or outsourced its capacity to care. The loss of community competence is the price we pay for the growth of the service economy."[2] They argue: "There is a colonizing dimension of professionalizing a capacity. It leaves us believing that only the certified professional has the capacity to help us with our troubles."[3] McKnight and Block would summon the unused capacities of laypersons. But if developing capacities was also the work of more professionals, they might find that they too have unused personal talents beyond their credentialed expertise. It is not an either/or proposition.

The prevailing assumption in academe is that students are deficient in what they know, and are taught with little attention paid to the capacities they bring with them to the classroom.[4] For example, there is little regard for the extensive work and community experience of students arriving at or returning to the classroom. The expectation of student or client deference is taken for granted by the professional mind-set, ignoring or even rejecting the unused capacities of those being served. Furthermore, the habit of deference is rarely examined when professional service is extended more broadly to help a neighborhood, association, or community find solutions for their problems. Deference means delegation instead of collaboration. Chapter 4 examined how treating knowledge as a social construct increasingly makes room for and encourages new layperson habits—the development of individual and group capacities that sometimes entirely bypass professionals who are not expecting nor encouraging layperson participation in knowledge production. And Chapter 5 argues that potluck deliberation could take advantage of professionals' expertise *and* citizen experience—both bringing their respective contributions to the table. "Capacity" is not just about individual potential, but how such potential can be developed and enlarged when working with others. Eric Raymond concluded that Linus Torvald's success with Linux and "open source" was a result of treating his "beta testers" as if they were his most valuable resource, and they responded by becoming just that.[5] And there is the example of the Industrial Areas Foundation, a network of community-based organizations that has developed the capacities of those helping to shape various social agendas. The foundation's cardinal rule is "never do anything for someone that they can do for themselves."[6]

Developing individual capacity is not the same as the hype about individual "empowerment," which is a misnomer. Empowerment is essentially a collective goal. Peter Levine, director of the CIRCLE Research Center at Tufts University, thinks of it as "public making." Levine cites John Dewey's conception of a "public" as "a group of citizens who have developed the capacity to define, debate, learn, and collectively address social problems." Levine concludes that: "'public making' presumably means increasing such capacity."[7] The self-reliant model in academe just does not address the powerlessness that so many graduates experience, despite their hard-won and costly professional credentials, which they assumed would be empowering. The self-reliant, credentialed model is driven, in part, by the admirable desire to be useful in an ever-changing public world, but such a model represents a failure of social imagination to explore what that public world might become when those with or without credentials work together as equals. Unfortunately, the culture of professionalism too often stresses individual achievement, ignoring shared social life—rendering service rather than developing collective capacity. It follows that professional competence, which assumes client deficiency, rarely considers the potential that collective capacity is one way to compensate for individual deficiency. When organizations and professionals hold themselves out to help customers and clients, economic self-interest too often precludes tapping the unused capacities of those to be served. Developing capacities, not just addressing deficiencies, would be a sea change in professional services. And it would eventually have to be made evident in institutional practices as well.[8]

Developing one's own capacities, however, is not necessarily the choice of those consumers who are busy doing other things. Time can be precious, which is one reason why the culture of professionalism remains relatively untouched. I think of my own example when waiting to hear from my computer consultant about a password change prompted by a Google warning that a hacker had tried to access my account. I don't understand how this happened, but with my consultant's help the password was changed in a "safe" manner, and I went about my business without wanting or needing to know how my consultant fixed things. I have to admit that there are many professional services that I don't think require any capacity development on my part at all—that is, if I can afford to pay for such service. Like many others I offer the usual, but careless, excuse that "it's beyond me," which is often nothing more than an unwillingness to understand what is unfamiliar and might require my time and attention. So for one reason or another, we often remain content to be consumers of what professionals can do for us rather than finding ways to become less dependent. A study of patients in the San Francisco Bay area found that they shared a common perception that primary care physicians "often acted authoritarian, rather than authoritative," but the study also noted that most of the patients "had either attended or completed graduate school." It seems that neither the physicians nor the patients had taken the time to discover that working together might better serve their respective interests.[9]

"New Professionals" from Academe

There are numerous examples of the emergence of a class of "new professionals" from academe; individuals who go out of their way to help nurture both citizen and community capacities. I draw here on what I have learned in the past twenty years co-editing the Kettering Foundation's *Higher Education Exchange* (*HEX*). The philosophy of *HEX* can be summed up in Thomas Jefferson's comment: "I know of no safe depository of the ultimate powers of the society but the people themselves; and if we think them not enlightened enough to exercise their control with a wholesome discretion, the remedy is not to take it from them, but to inform their discretion by education."[10] Kettering and *HEX* focus on fostering a more democratic culture, which is certainly not what the culture of professionalism headquartered in academe has been concerned with since its ascendance in the twentieth century. A democratic culture assumes there is a rough equality among all those who take part—professionals and citizens—in helping to solve social problems. A democratic culture does not reject what credentialed experts have to offer, but when citizens share their experience and judgment they also bring their individual and collective capacities to bear on mutual problems. Fortunately, such capacities are being encouraged by "new professionals" from academe in many different ways to help develop a democratic culture far different from the prevailing culture of professionalism.

Who are these new professionals? Harry Boyte at Augsburg College is one of America's premier mechanics servicing the engine of participatory democracy. A social progressive immersed in the civil rights struggles of the 1960s, Boyte moved on from that era to become a social theorist but remained a practical organizer. For years Boyte has tinkered with democracy's underside, and like a good mechanic he has offered fixes and installed practices to keep the engine running. Boyte has never given up on the potential of collective action on the part of ordinary citizens, even as he has had to account for the enormous reach and influence of America's culture of professionalism. He has used the lesson of American history again and again to confirm for himself and others that such collective action in the form of "democratic movements" remains ever possible, despite being increasingly circumscribed by the professional "service" world. With Sara Evans, one of Boyte's early contributions to the ongoing dialogue about participatory democracy was articulating the concept of "free spaces"—those voluntary forms of association where citizens learn about their collective potential—a kind of middle ground between their "private lives and large-scale institutions."[11]

Perhaps Boyte's most important and enduring effort to keep democracy's engine running has been his concept of "public work." For Boyte, "public work" is the "unfinished work of the people" grounded in a challenge that citizenship should be far more than just voting and volunteering. Along the way, Boyte has been critical of how little academe has been part of such work. For Boyte, public work "helps get professionals back in the mix of everyday experience and common life." Referring to the apparent "objective" detachment of academe, Boyte told me, "I like 'public work' because it discomfits those who want to maintain distance."[12] Boyte remains optimistic about those in academe finding ways to engage with citizens in public work. He told me of a "palpable hunger for more public experiences" based on interviews he conducted with senior faculty at the University of Minnesota.[13] Albert Dzur, another new kind of professional in academe, told me that his term "democratic professionalism" addresses such hunger and offers "an alternative understanding of public accountability more congruent with traditional conceptions of the university as a cooperative community of knowledge seekers. Collaborating with lay people and allowing professional practices to be open to critical reflection from outsiders . . . are ways of narrowing the social distance between campuses and wider communities."[14]

Over the years, Boyte's "public work" concept has moved to several sites in academe. For example, Adam Weinberg, now president of Denison University, was at the center of "public work" at Colgate University when he was Dean of the College and a professor of sociology. When I talked then with Weinberg, he saw "public work" as "a seven-year process to rebuild campus life at Colgate around the principle of 'civic learning.'" It started with Colgate's partnership with the village and town of Hamilton in upstate New York, where the university resides. It focused on economic development, but then led to many different initiatives on campus, since Weinberg saw "public work" as an ongoing process of civic education on campus, not just in town/gown relationships. It meant "creating a more entrepreneurial culture where students would think of themselves as innovators, creators, and problem solvers." So at Weinberg's urging the university moved away from a "professional service model" of staff being the problem solvers for students, making students little more than "customers or guests." Instead, the "public work" model helped students "to think of themselves as members of a community" who had the responsibility "to work with others to create a healthy living environment." When I asked Weinberg for a campus example, without hesitation he said it was in the residential halls—"a diversity of students" in "small spaces." He told me that "we have learned to use conflicts" that arise in the residence halls "as opportunities to help students learn to do public work . . . that community starts in the small democratic actions that people take in the everyday" that can happen anywhere whether on campus or off. In an interesting aside, Weinberg told me that resistance to Colgate's public work effort came from parents who thought of academe as a place to purchase "a set of services" and to make their children "happy and professionally successful." Weinberg saw a continuing challenge in "taking students who have grown up in non-civic communities and to equip them with the capacity to be citizens, community organizers, and democratic leaders."[15] Weinberg, now at Denison, argues: "public work is the defining outcome we are aiming for when we talk about civic education and community engagement efforts. Our students have the desire and ambitions, but lack the capacity to do public work." Weinberg would prepare students "to shift the professional from somebody who acts on us to somebody who acts with us." Weinberg would have students move "beyond volunteerism to public work." He added: "We need to become co-learners who work with, not on, local communities."[16]

Where Adam Weinberg saw residence halls as the best places to teach the "arts of public work," other efforts in academe put students into communities that develop both the capacities of the students to do public work and the capacities of those with whom they work. There is the work of Mark Wilson and Nan Fairley with undergraduates at Auburn University in Alabama. Wilson is coordinator of community and civic engagement in the College of Liberal Arts at Auburn, and Fairley is a professor of journalism. The focus of Wilson and Fairley is on "Living Democracy," a project that they have shaped and pursued that involves Auburn students collaborating with local communities across Alabama. Each student lives in a community over a summer and co-creates a project with those in the community that is intended to build the capacities of those living there, including the student's. Unlike professional consultants, who come and go, students live in a community to better understand what can be done and by whom to make it a better place. Living Democracy is a far different approach from what Wilson and Farley describe as academe's focus on "citizens and communities as either research subjects or consumers of products and services."[17] A Living Democracy fellow has no predetermined agenda when he or she arrives in a community. The point is to learn about a community's problems and possibilities, and then find ways to work with community partners who can help make things happen. As David Mathews of the Kettering Foundation describes the project: "Students 'enroll' in community just as they enroll in the academic department where they major."[18] A humanities scholar recently cited with approval for me the Auburn project: "The relationship among terms like 'community service,' 'service professions' . . . helpfully complicates professionalism."[19]

Marguerite (Peggy) Shaffer, a professor of American Studies at Miami University of Ohio, created the "Acting Locally" program so students could help build civic capacities—others' and their own. Like so many from academe whom I have interviewed, Shaffer has tried to counter the "privatization" of students and citizens alike with the possibilities of their collaborative learning, which has been sorely neglected. With "Acting Locally," Shaffer sought to create and sustain "trusting partnerships" between students and community members. Students in the program do not seek to provide answers for social problems but rather "sharing resources and knowledge" and "privileging public work."[20] Shaffer has experienced the problem in academe of both faculty and students wanting outcomes "easily documented and measured," which "works against the need to be open-ended in community partnership work."[21] Like so many professionals in academe who have experienced the restraints and limitations of their on-campus lives, Shaffer once questioned whether she was pursuing the right course for her life. By doing work beyond academe with students who have not yet been captured by the culture of professionalism, it seems Shaffer has used Acting Locally to correct the imbalance. Back then she told me poignantly: "I have joked with colleagues that I am in the midst of an academic mid-life crisis—questioning every aspect of life in academe . . . I have questioned the time I devote to teaching critical thinking skills to students who are socialized, both inside and outside the university, to care more about their final grades and potential career options than the knowledge they can share and the collective future they can create."[22] Like many of her students, Shaffer found room to be a cultural agent, and her work in American Studies is a piece with what she learned from her Acting Locally work—a "partnership mechanism" for "culture making . . . the act of coming together . . . that brings publics into being" with students seeing themselves "as participants in a public process."[23]

There is also the work of Ellen Knutson and Dan Lewis who developed the Graduate Engagement Opportunities (GEO) Community Practicum program at Northwestern University. The GEO program has graduate students "undertake a quarter-long practicum or field study in the overlapping areas of civic engagement, social justice, or community studies."[24] The program involves graduate students working with various community organizations in nearby Chicago. Knutson and Lewis have said such work enlarges student capacities "beyond their narrow disciplinary knowledge. They . . . learn how to navigate the complex and often rocky terrain of community relationships and collaborative inquiry." For Northwestern, "the GEO program models how a research university can begin to reform doctoral education."[25] Knutson, no longer at Northwestern, and Lewis hope the program can "reinvigorate doctoral education" as well as "contribute to the health of the communities that surround institutions of higher learning."[26] The program also gives more career options to those who participate at a time when finding work outside of academe has sometimes become more necessary but which sometimes can also be more attractive.

Harry Boyte's concept of public work reaches far beyond academe, but he has not neglected the central role that academe can play if it were to do more as an "agent of democracy." For Boyte, too much of academe is "technocratic," meaning "a politics without a name, presenting itself as an objective set of truths, practices, and procedures."[27] Boyte has consistently argued that the "technocratic-expert approach" to solving public problems "simply doesn't work."[28] For Boyte, "public work" counters the culture of professionalism that resides in academe. Repeatedly, he uses the phrase "experts on tap not on top."[29] Boyte points to three needed changes in academe. "We need political education that challenges abstractions and teaches work attentive to context and particularities of interests and backgrounds. We need organizing for cultural change in our professions and institutions to reground them in living contexts. And we need a broader political and strategic framework that shifts scholarly attention from what is wrong to the primary question, what solves problems in ways that build democratic society?"[30] It is what some might think of as "the public's work."

Recently, Boyte took on the added responsibility of being the national coordinator for the American Commonwealth Partnership (ACP), a year-long project in 2012 of the White House Office of Public Engagement, the Department of Education, the Association of American Colleges and Universities, and the Campaign for the Civic Mission of the Schools. The ACP alliance worked to promote the "democracy college ideal" with students learning "skills of working across differences on public problems" in nearby communities. With the National Issues Forums, ACP helped to launch "a national discussion on higher education's role in America's future"—typical of Boyte's ambition to bring academe and citizens into close, working relationships.[31]

For years, Boyte's work was centered at the University of Minnesota as coordinator of the Center for Democracy and Citizenship. More recently Boyte moved the Center to Augsburg College. But Boyte's interests remain far-flung. Recently, he told me about the Citizen Alum effort, led by Julie Ellison at the University of Michigan, that "reconceives alumni as partners in connections with communities and in teaching and learning, not only as donors." Boyte also cited Northern Arizona University, which now introduces its students to "public work experiences," and the Delta Center at the University of Iowa that has pursued "civic science," bringing citizens and scientists together to share "their diverse kinds of knowledge and talents . . . to do public work that solves problems."[32] Broadly speaking, Boyte would have the "skills and habits of civic politics include relationship building, tolerance for ambiguity, ability to deal with conflict constructively, and the capacity to act in open environments with no predetermined outcomes. These are not part of normal higher education curricula . . . The capacities for civic politics and civic professionalism have to be learned mainly in practice, and they also entail unlearning tendencies such as the bent for hypercompetitive individualism, the posture of intellectual certitude, and the stance of outside observer learned in conventional graduate education."[33] Boyte is not one to leave any stone unturned, showing inexhaustible idealism to put democracy's engine in high gear.

"Public" or "engaged" scholarship, associated with the concept of "public work," is another undertaking in academe that has many dimensions and stories to tell. Scott Peters at Cornell University, a scholar of the American land-grant history, has pursued how those in academe, both professionals and students, "engage with their non-academic partners in the public work of naming and framing problems [and] deciding what should be done about them."[34] Jeremy Cohen, the founder of Penn State's Laboratory for Public Scholarship and Democracy, has seen the challenge: "Successful public scholarship requires an educational apprenticeship steeped in the disciplinary acquisition of knowledge and the incremental development of democratic judgment and skill, and like any new and complex capacity, democracy does not come naturally. It is learned."[35] Julie Ellison, at the University of Michigan, reminded me recently that the idea of public scholarship has always been "situated" in the "broader notion of public work."[36] Ellison is the founder of Imagining America and, among other initiatives, has pursued a "Tenure Team Initiative on Public Scholarship" centered on tenure and promotion policies that "lag behind public scholarly and creative work and discourage faculty from doing it."[37] Ellison, however, told me that the challenge posed by linking public scholarship to tenure remains "intermittent and episodic" given "the goals and aspirations . . . of contract or contingent instructors."[38] Only twenty-five percent of academics are tenured or on tenure tracks.

The Legacy of Jane Addams

A dramatic example of a capacity enabler is Jane Addams and her colleagues at Hull-House in Chicago who, at the turn of the twentieth century, engaged those in the immigrant neighborhood of Hull-House as equals. It was a remarkable contrast to the ascending professional culture around them at the University of Chicago and elsewhere in the city. As citizens sought to come to terms with the immigrant influx of their day, Lawrence Cremin tells of both settlement houses and Salvationists in the late nineteenth and early twentieth centuries sharing "a commitment to the crucial role of education in rebuilding communities rent by the forces of industrialization." The Salvation Army "conveyed knowledge, taught skills, redirected aspirations, and changed behavior." Jane Addams's Hull-House offered "picture exhibitions, university extension classes, and special lectures, as well as engaging in political activities on behalf of public libraries, parks, playgrounds and schools." What began as Hull-House staff reading to the first visitors from the neighborhood led to the study of texts "with their neighbors" in what Cremin describes as "reciprocal interpretation." Cremin goes on: "Instead of drawing educational functions unto itself . . . [Hull-House] reached out into the community to help organize social relations in such a way that the community itself would become educative." From the example of Hull-House and the settlement house movement came "the visiting nurse, the visiting teacher, the child guidance clinic, the child-care center, the community recreation center, and the senior citizens' center . . . and a new educational profession, social work."[39]

William Sullivan saw Addams's enabling mission as "linked to the broad social view of participation and trust among citizens which she called democracy." According to Sullivan: "By integrating her clients into a professionally sustained community of work, education, and discussion, Addams sought to make possible their development as active and responsible family members, workers, and citizens."[40] For Addams, democracy assumed a rough equality in public life, at least among citizens who wanted to take part in addressing public problems—together. Equality of talent? No. Equality of means? No. But equality to participate with and learn from others, sharing whatever gifts one had with the group. "Addams thought of those who came and went at Hull-House as citizens or citizens in the making, not as clients or receivers of services."[41] Doing good for others? No. Doing good *with* others? Yes.[42] Jane Addams possessed a remarkable faith in the potential of those she worked with, as together they would use all their "unrealized and unevoked capacity."[43] As Louis Menand noted: "She found that people she was trying to help had better ideas about how their lives might be improved than she and her colleagues did."[44]

The Hull-House example reminds me that the desire for the exercise of authority is often characteristic of men, whether as professors or practicing professionals, but it seems less the preference of women who are professionals. It has been my experience that the nonhierarchical examples of women, in whatever "professional" category one can imagine, have contributed to collaborative learning in classrooms, workplaces, and communities. I have noted elsewhere, "that what I learned about problem solving in my classrooms, semester after semester and year after year, was the example of women in their respective work groups helping the group work—together . . . I think the century-old story of what it means to be a professional is bound to change when altered and enlarged by the example of women."[45] When I mentioned to MaryAnn Murphy, Associate Professor of Communication Studies at Pace University, my observation that women seemed more than ready to reject or modify a professional mind-set that had been crafted by men, she said: "There was a time when women who wanted a professional life felt that the only way to make it was to work off the male model and try and think and behave like men. The research has shown quite clearly that such tactics did not work out well for women . . . I think we can allow our differences to be our strengths. For instance, one interesting research finding is that women are the problem solvers in the workplace."[46]

From time to time, I have been chastised by those who essentially agree with my observations about professional women being capacity builders, but are quite emphatic that my gender disqualifies me from pursuing the subject. I have insisted, however, that it is a subject that should interest anyone and everyone who thinks the example of women in sufficient numbers has the potential of bringing about significant change. I would argue that nurturing others' capacities, which is lacking among so many practicing professionals, comes far more naturally to women than to men. In her work thirty years ago, Carol Gilligan saw how professional training confused what most women valued in themselves. "If anything, they regard their professional activities as jeopardizing their own sense of themselves, and the conflict they encounter between achievement and care leaves them either divided in judgment or feeling betrayed."[47] It follows then that women are less likely to define themselves, as men do, as strictly "professionals." Consequently, women as professionals are more likely to engage all their talents, not just their expertise. They are less likely to define and limit what they have to offer. Social entrepreneur Allison Fine concludes: "The innate ability of many women to connect, share information, and collaborate will serve them well in this new age."[48] I learned from KerryAnn O'Meara, a professor of higher education at the University of Maryland, that "women and minorities self-report on surveys being disproportionately interested in areas of study with direct social relevance, which is why the NSF [National Science Foundation] has encouraged the disciplines in science, technology, engineering, and mathematics to integrate community engagement into their undergraduate and graduate programs to attract these groups."[49]

Collaborative learning does not depend on someone's authority. It depends on everyone's capacity to contribute. When a professional tries to help someone get up, that someone has to make an effort to get up with the professional's help. From my professional experience beyond the classroom, such professional help seems to come more naturally from women, who may have experienced, at one time or another, what it means to be down, or to be put down, and how much effort is required to get up. New knowledge from many different sources indicates that women in particular are potential capacity enablers. Sally Helgesen notes their "focus on process rather than on achievement or closure." They "get pleasure from the actual doing . . . rather than from the abstract notion of getting it done."[50] What many professional women choose to ignore or put aside is the professional habit of setting oneself apart from those who are to be served. Nurturing everyone's capacities seems to come easier to credentialed women, as they put themselves more at the center among relative equals rather than standing apart—a distance maintained by some professional men who may seek to gain others' deference. According to Linda Coughlin: "For most women power is derived from a 'power within,' or a 'power with' as opposed to a 'power over'—a hierarchical paradigm."[51]

Kenneth Bruffee took note in *Collaborative Learning*, that "autonomous peer groups" were, at one time, "the only education resource available to women." Bruffee goes on to say that more recently women have acquired "the impetus, experience, and expertise gained in support groups developed by the women's movement."[52] Support groups are often put together and kept together by women, professional or not, who focus on other people's gifts, not just their needs. Such gifts initially belong to individuals but really only become gifts when they are offered to others, and no credentials are required to offer something of value.[53]

Today, in the spirit of Jane Addams, there is a Jane Addams School for Democracy (JAS) in St. Paul, Minnesota, which has brought together those in academe with the local Hmong, Latino, and East African immigrant communities. JAS is a partnership that involves students and faculty from several area colleges and universities. JAS has also brought together those "with a vision to create a democratic organization and egalitarian way of working and learning across cultures."[54] Capacity building is shared where the "distinction between learners and teachers blur. We all teach. We all learn. Every person has something of value to contribute."[55] There are currently four learning exchange circles that were organized by the participants and include individuals from a variety of ethnic backgrounds. There are many other activities at JAS—neighborhood art and theater projects with children, a community wellness project, and civic work on "new policy initiatives for citizenship, health care, transportation and housing." Participants at JAS "see themselves primarily as contributors rather than as clients or recipients of services."[56]

JAS differs from but has strong ties to academe. Students do not strictly serve the communities, but instead work with them as collaborators. No doubt there are problems in such a civic arrangement. Students "familiar with the service learning framework and the primacy of academic knowledge" sometimes struggle to adapt. Nonetheless, as newcomers they are asked "simply to find membership in a diverse community."[57] JAS's organization and practices are very similar to those at Jane Addams's Hull-House, which arose at the time when professionalism was ascending in academe. Professionalism's trajectory had little in common with the practices of a settlement house and still has little in common with JAS. Yet the nurturing of capacities of both immigrants and approximately six hundred participating students is an interesting model of how America's culture of professionalism might change. Addams believed that "people could learn to be bold, confident, public-spirited actors with skills for self-governance and capacities to co-create a robust common world through their labor."[58] Nan Skelton and Nan Kari, co-founders of JAS, helped to develop a culture that "emerged organically" from the practices they introduced, similar to what Jane Addams had shared with immigrants a century before. Together Skelton and Kari found: "It has called for a debunking of myths that many of us have learned in our own professional socialization."[59] It follows then that, as founders, their own capacities have been extended and enlarged as well.

At a time when immigrant policies have been fiercely debated "inside the Beltway," the JAS story offers a positive example of how interests can be reconciled while furthering the "unfinished business of democracy." Nan Kari sees JAS as "a laboratory to better understand the core ideas and practices of public work, a practical theory of democracy."[60] Here Harry Boyte's concept and influence have been realized by the progress made by JAS since 1996. JAS considers itself a liberator of everyone's "talents and energies—what Jane Addams called 'freeing the powers.'"[61] Such liberation is seen as necessary to overcome the limitations that many well-meaning professionals impose on those they serve. In the JAS enterprise, knowledge is not delivered to others but created with them. Whatever the participants eventually learn is embedded in the process they share. Kettering Foundation's David Mathews observed that at JAS they have to "make the road by walking"; there is no predetermined path or destination.[62] Consequently, students and some faculty cross over to new territories of learning that little resemble what goes on in traditional classrooms. And it is no coincidence that the origins and heavy lifting in such an alternative enterprise come from the efforts of women professionals, working with those from academe and neighborhood members as equals. Such "new professionals" are indeed capacity enablers.

Culture Change?

Intellect, presumably at the heart of professionalism, may be less important in culture change than new ways of "acting professionally." Professionalism is something still evolving, and the work of "new professionals" says as much, as they find new ways of nurturing capacities—their own and those they try to serve. Although the culture of professionalism may appear to be comfortably settled with strong institutional supports, those who enter and reside in that status quo are not necessarily settled themselves. Perhaps Philip Slater's 1960s insight still applies when considering the possibility of an individual's conversion "from one orientation to its exact opposite," which may appear to be a "gross change" but "actually involves only a very small shift in the balance of a focal and persistent conflict."[63] "New professionals" from academe appear to be just such converts—to see themselves anew and to rethink America's culture of professionalism.

Significant culture change, however, will not come easily. I recall James Buchanan's warning that "any proposal for change involves the status quo as the necessary starting point. 'We start from here,' and not . . . someplace else."[64] Furthermore, culture change is not within the grasp of any one individual or group of individuals, and there certainly is no foreordained or prescribed path. How does culture change occur? I think the key is to find a simple melody; people can't hum a complicated tune.

So, is culture change possible? It will take enough others finding new ways of acting "professionally" and discovering from collaborative learning, online or elsewhere, that knowledge is a social construct, not a form of property. It will take enough others learning to trust their own experience with everyone having something to offer in any potluck deliberation with experts and nurturing the capacities of those they serve rather than prolonging their dependence. Besides, the social landscape is already changing with citizens and professionals finding new and different ways to learn from each other. Perhaps my argument throughout this book can contribute in some way to further such a change, or perhaps it will take some precipitating event or events that will produce a sea change, which no one now can foresee. In any event, it will take "enough others"—*both* those who are professionals and those who are not. When weaving new nets, all threads count.

"A Bunch of Amateurs" (II)

Nathan Sax, the president of Pennacook University, could not help smiling when he saw who shared the platform at the university's commencement ceremony. Next to Harry Frank, a trustee and Pennacook's investment adviser, was Jenny Stackhouse, the valedictorian but also a leader of Students for Divestment Now (SDN). Frank had told Sax, as far as selling the stock that Pennacook owned in fossil-fuel companies, "you can't afford to listen to a bunch of amateurs." Now Harry Frank leaned over and whispered in Sax's good ear, "Maybe, with Ms. Stackhouse moving on, things will get back to normal, whatever 'normal' means." Sax frankly had never experienced "normal" at Pennacook.

When it came time for Jenny's remarks, she rose and proceeded to the lectern and microphone, then turned to Sax. In an exaggerated stage whisper she could be heard to say: "President Sax, SDN is not graduating today—just me and some friends. We may be a 'bunch of amateurs,' but we don't give up that easily." How she had learned of Harry Frank's remarks, Sax would never know. Anyway, Jenny received a smattering of applause from those in attendance who heard her whispered aside to Pennacook's president. Sax winced but smiled and then waved to no one in particular. He thought, why would this young woman with a first-rate mind and a promising future among America's elites be so fixed on climate change? Maybe he should recommend her for the young alum slot on the trustee board. Sax had to admit he admired her spirit.

Jenny Stackhouse was just getting started. After a courteous acknowledgement of all those in attendance, she spoke without notes: "As graduating seniors, we have had many opportunities to see that perhaps the education of 'amateurs,'" with that she turned to the president again, winked, and continued: "the education of amateurs may be the best hope of producing the kind of citizens and leaders that our country needs to renew the vitality of our private and public institutions. Where else will the vision come from?" Stackhouse paused and then answered her own question. "Surely, not from professionals alone."

Sax smiled at Harry Frank who did not seem amused. Stackhouse continued. "I would start at those places in academe that are willing to help students see the limitations of professional life and explore amateur alternatives. The education of amateurs does not foreclose the option of specialization and a professional career, but it does offer the possibility of finding a different kind of personal fulfillment.

"Amateurs never learn professional manners. They learn that ignorance is the starting point of any intellectual enterprise. They learn how to use their ignorance in any field of knowledge. For example, 'doing' science was first the avocation of amateurs who only wanted to look for themselves rather than rely on the preconceived ideas of others. Modern amateurs also 'do' science to learn that its finished products do not explain or even resemble the creative process that brought them into existence. Their work is not original or elegant, but they learn what it means to produce knowledge instead of only learning what someone else's knowledge means.

"Amateurs have no ambition to make a living on someone else's property, but they have the curiosity and confidence to ask hard questions. They are not passive consumers." On this note, Jenny was interrupted by some applause. She smiled and went on: "In professional fields staked out with 'no trespassing' signs, they are gentle intruders. Everywhere they go, amateurs ask the professional, 'Don't tell us what you know, please tell us how you came to know it. How do you produce your knowledge? What do you actually do in your office or study or laboratory? Describe to us your methods with a vocabulary that we can share and tell us in words that we can understand. And, if you have time, please tell us what you don't know.' All that may take a lifetime, but what better reason do amateurs need?"

Jenny seemed to be warming up. "Amateurs can help themselves and others to make room for their personal values as an important basis for their participation in a culture preoccupied with the production, distribution, and consumption of credentialed knowledge. We may be novices, but amateurs pursue interests and causes for their own sake, for the love of something that has little or nothing to do with an acquired credential. Amateurs never hide behind a professional mask. They offer themselves rather than their credentials and use the gift of their moral imagination to determine where they are most needed. They reject the notion that their college or university is nothing more than neutral ground for their preferences and entitlements. They want the 'communities' on campus to be more than therapeutic. Since they do not yet have credentials, they work at helping others without pretense or detachment. As a result, amateurs never have to measure their own worth according to professional standards of 'objectivity' or 'cognitive efficiency.' Such conceits leave too much out and may leave too many people out. Amateurs make room in public life for private commitments, idealism, passion, zeal, indignation, and feeling, and by their example they make room for everyone, educated or not, employed or unemployed, young or old, who has a gift and who wants to participate in all that needs doing."

Jenny took a deep breath: "In 1869 Charles Eliot, the new president of Harvard, set higher education on a new road towards professional specialization. He foresaw a 'national danger' in the 'vulgar conceit that a Yankee can turn his hand to anything.' Today I think our country faces a new danger. The intellectual and moral example of the professionalized university does not adequately serve the needs of young women and men or the future of a democratic society. It is time that we educated what Mr. Eliot might call a 'bunch of amateurs.'"

To a generous round of applause and a few "whoops" from Jenny's friends, she returned to take her seat next to Harry Frank.

Now it was the president's turn, a man of few words on such occasions, but of many words in his philosophy class, which he still found time to fit in between his many presidential excursions to raise money for Pennacook. Sax turned and thanked Ms. Stack-house for her "thoughtful" remarks. Now it was his turn, and everyone knew he wouldn't take long at the lectern.

Pointing to the fresh band aid on his forehead, Sax began:

"The young surgeon in the emergency room last Friday asked me: 'Why do you rollerblade?'

"I looked up: 'I'm 64 and I need the workout.'

"Then he looked down at me: 'Don't you think you should act your age?' And I laughed: '"Over my dead body.'

"Then he said: 'That's what I'm talking about.'

"I started reciting Dylan Thomas, 'Rage, rage against the dying of the light.'

"And he just laughed and started sewing me up.

"A bad tumble, however, has a strange way of clearing the head, of reducing one's thoughts to essential things . . . like standing up, lying down and getting through the night.

"What does any university honor on this occasion? Obviously, the knowledge it conveys and your acquisition of it. We are proud, as you are, of your accomplishment. Your friends and families who are here are proud, too. Good for us, all of us. The world needs our knowledge. Do we need more knowledge? Of course! Is knowledge enough? We know it isn't. Does it get us through the night? We rather doubt it."

Sax paused, then took a deep breath, "But in a university setting, we usually only honor certain gifts. We rarely acknowledge the power and need for love—the gift of love. It is here . . . but hushed or overlooked or lacking the requisite discipline. It has nothing to do with theory but everything to do with practice. It has nothing to do with efficiency, but everything to do with social justice. It has nothing to do with your credentials, but everything to do with how you choose to use them.

"Does the world need more knowledge? Of course! Does the world need more love? This is how the writer, Wendell Berry, put it: 'All the grand and perfect dreams of the technologists are happening in the future, but nobody is there. What can turn us from the deserted future, back into the sphere of our being, the great dance that joins us to our home, to each other and to other creatures, to the dead and the unborn? I think it is love.'"

Sax paused, "I think so too. I think it gets us—all of us—through the night."

Looking out at the assembled graduates, Sax paused again: "The world desperately needs your talent, your knowledge . . . and your love. When you can, come back and tell us how it's going."

With that, Sax walked over to Jenny Stackhouse, who stood applauding, and in an awkward but well-meant gesture gave her a big hug.

Notes

Introduction

1. Eva T. H. Brann, *Paradoxes of Education in a Republic* (University of Chicago Press, 1979), 39. Further on, Brann would have citizens in a republic "thinking things anew rather than . . . thinking new things" (106). Furthermore, Steven Brint indicates that "the label 'professional' . . . can be refashioned periodically to suit an evolving social and cultural context." *In the Age of Experts: The Changing Role of Professionals in Politics and Public Life* (Princeton University Press, 1994), 8.
2. Edna Ullmann-Margalit, *The Emergence of Norms* (Oxford University Press, 1977) 76.
3. Ibid., 8.
4. Robert Sugden, "Spontaneous Order," *Journal of Economic Perspectives* 3, 4 (Fall, 1989): 93.
5. Edgar H. Schein, *The Corporate Culture Survival Guide: Sense and Nonsense About Culture Change* (Jossey-Bass, 1999), 41, 43, 46. Schein identified assumptions that characterize organizational culture, but they also apply in professional precincts.
6. Louis Menand, *The Metaphysical Club: A Story of Ideas in America* (Farrar, Straus and Giroux, 2001), 415.
7. Brint, *In the Age of Experts*, 7.
8. Jacques Barzun, "The Professions Under Siege," *Harpers* (October 1978): 65.
9. Burton Clark, *The Higher Education System: Academic Organization in Cross-National Perspective* (University of California Press, 1983), 116.
10. Thomas L. Haskell, *The Emergence of Professional Social Science: The American Social Science Association and the Nineteenth-Century Crisis of Authority* (Johns Hopkins University Press, 1977), 27.
11. William S. Sullivan, *Work and Integrity: The Crisis and Promise of Professionalism in America* (HarperCollins, 1995), 2.
12. Harold Wilensky, "The Professionalization of Everyone?" *The American Journal of Sociology* LXX, 2 (September 1964): 149.

13. Michael Polanyi, "Tacit Knowing: Its Bearing on Some Problems of Philosophy," *Review of Modern Physics* 34 (October, 1962): 601.
14. Michael Walzer, *Spheres of Justice: A Defense of Pluralism and Equality* (Basic Books, 1983), 156.
15. Mary Ann Murphy/Brown email 5/30/13.
16. Walker Percy, *The Message in the Bottle* (Farrar, Straus and Giroux, 1977), 22. A former colleague of mine, Jackson Kytle, wrote: "[E]ducation has gone too far by banishing the personal voice . . . one symptom of the tyranny of scientific reductionism in intellectual circles is the loss of the personal." *To Want to Learn: Insights and Provocations for Engaged Learning* (Palgrave Macmillan, 2004), p. xvi.

Chapter 1

1. Emerson would also champion those with "knowledge." Burton J. Bledstein, *The Culture of Professionalism: The Middle Class and the Development of Higher Education in America* (W.W. Norton, 1978), 266.
2. As described by Stuart Banner, "Property is not an end in itself but rather a means to many other ends. . . . From the abandonment of feudal land tenure in colonial times to the expansion of copyright at the time of the twenty-first century, our ideas about property have always been in flux." *American Property: A History of How, Why, and What We Own* (Harvard University Press, 2011), 289–90.
3. Quoted in Jedediah Purdy, *The Meaning of Property: Freedom, Community, and the Legal Imagination* (Yale University Press, 2010), 1. Purdy adds: "Land made a person substantial" (59).
4. Alexis de Tocqueville, *Democracy in America*, trans. George Lawrence, ed. J. P. Mayer (Doubleday Anchor Books, 1969), 638–39. According to Sean Wilentz, in America's founding and early expansion the argument was made forcefully that "the possession of property helped temper the disruptive passions and weaknesses common to all mankind." *The Rise of American Democracy: Jefferson to Lincoln* (W. W. Norton, 2005), 343.
5. Robert H. Wiebe, *Self-Rule: A Cultural History of American Democracy* (University of Chicago Press, 1995), 39.
6. Wilentz, *Rise of American Democracy*, 16.
7. Richard Flacks, *Making History: The American Left and the American Mind* (Columbia University Press, 1988), 9.
8. Purdy, *Meaning of Property*, 17.
9. Bledstein, *Culture of Professionalism*, 92. Samuel Haber put it succinctly: "Professions . . . offer a way of life." *The Quest for Authority and Honor in the American Professions, 1750–1900* (University of Chicago Press, 1991), 36.

10. John Dewey, *The Quest for Certainty* (G. P. Putnam's Sons, 1979), 217. Dewey also argued, "the notion that intelligence is a personal endowment or personal attainment is the great conceit of the intellectual class, as that of the commercial class that wealth is something which they personally have wrought and possess." *The Public and Its Problems* (Swallow Press, 1988), 211.

11. John McKnight and Peter Block, *The Abundant Community: Awakening the Power of Families and Neighborhoods* (Berrett-Koehler, 2010), 28. On the other hand, some Americans distrust expert authority when it comes to critical issues such as climate change. Christopher Hayes, a rhetorical slayer of America's "elites," argues that "the fundamental problem is that too many Americans simply don't trust the various forms of scientific and elite authority through which information about the threat of climate change is transmitted." *The Twilight of the Elites: America After Meritocracy* (Crown, 2012), 136.

12. Banner, *American Property*, 20.

13. Isaiah Berlin quoted in Purdy, *Meaning of Property*, 19.

14. Brian Z. Tamanaha, *Failing Law Schools* (University of Chicago Press, 2012), 6. Taking the property analogy further, the academic departments in new universities of the late nineteenth century could be compared to the proliferation of "co-ops" in the 1920s, which homeowners assembled in one building or another in a big city, such as New York, that gave the resident "owners" the collective power to exclude any prospective buyer who did not suit them for one reason or another.

15. Banner, *American Property*, 26.

16. Bledstein, *Culture of Professionalism*, 323.

17. Wynne Wright, "Wicked Bedfellows: Can Science and Democracy Coexist in the Land Grant?" *Higher Education Exchange*, 2012, 60.

18. Thomas Haskell, *The Emergence of Professional Social Science*, 27.

19. Bledstein, *Culture of Professionalism*, 127.

20. Ibid., p. x.

21. David Damrosch, *We Scholars: Changing the Culture of the University* (Harvard University Press, 1995), 2.

22. Bledstein, *Culture of Professionalism*, 84.

23. Tamahana, *Failing Law Schools*, 21.

24. Bledstein, *Culture of Professionalism*, 277.

25. Tamahana, 84.

26. Bledstein, 271.

27. Thomas Bender, *Intellect and Public Life: Essays on the Social History of Academic Intellectuals in the United States* (Johns Hopkins University Press, 1993), 131.

28. Michael Polanyi and Harry Prosch: "The simple fact [is] that scientists keep watch over one another. Each scientist is both subject to criticism by all other scientists and encouraged by their appreciation of him. This is how the scientific opinion is formed which enforces scientific standards and regulates the distribution of professional opportunities." *Meaning* (University of Chicago Press), 191.

29. Quoted in Thomas Bender, "Politics, Intellect, and the American University, 1945–1995," in *American Academic Culture in Transformation: Fifty Years, Four Disciplines*, ed. Thomas Bender and Carl E. Schorske (Princeton University Press, 1997), 23.

30. Henry Rosovsky, *The University: An Owner's Manual* (W. W. Norton, 1990), 161.

31. David Cooper/Brown email 3/18/13.

32. Andrew Delbanco, *College: What It Was, Is, and Should Be* (Harvard University Press, 2012), 79–80.

33. Samuel Haber, *The Quest for Authority and Honor*, 293.

34. Albert W. Dzur, *Democratic Professionalism: Citizen Participation and the Reconstruction of Professional Ethics, Identity and Practice* (Pennsylvania State University Press, 2008), 45.

35. Bledstein, *Culture of Professionalism*, 96.

36. William S. Sullivan, *Work and Integrity: The Crisis and Promise of Porfessionalism in America* (HarperCollins, 1995), 37.

37. Bender and Schorske, *American Academic Culture in Transformation*, 21.

38. Laurence Veysey, *The Emergence of the American University* (University of Chicago Press, 1965), 337–338.

39. Gerald Graff, *Beyond the Culture Wars: How Teaching the Conflicts Can Revitalize American Education* (W.W. Norton, 1992), 137–138.

40. David Cooper/Brown email 3/18/13.

41. Julie Ellison/Brown email 9/6/13.

42. James Surowiecki, *The Wisdom of Crowds: Why the Many Are Smarter Than the Few and How Collective Wisdom Shapes Business, Economies, Societies and Nations* (Doubleday, 2004), 167.

43. Lee Benson, Ira Harkavy, and John Puckett, "Democratic Transformation Through University-Assisted Community Schools," in *"To Serve a Larger Purpose": Engagement for Democracy and the Transformation of Higher Education*, ed. John Saltmarsh and Matthew Hartley (Temple University Press, 2011), 67.

44. Elizabeth Minnich/Brown email 7/5/13.

45. Albert O. Hirschman, *Shifting Involvements: Private Interest and Public Action* (Princeton University Press, 1982), 81.

46. Thomas S. Kuhn, *The Structure of Scientific Revolutions*, 2nd ed. (University of Chicago Press, 1962), 90.

47. Robert K. Merton, *Social Theory and Social Structures,* enlarged ed. (Free Press, 1968), 4.

48. Duncan Watts, *Six Degrees: The Science of a Connected Age* (W.W. Norton, 2013), 14–15.

49. Donald Levine goes further: "Instead of minding the imperative to optimize the growth of students, most universities offer little or nothing to counter the interest of scholarly specialists or fractious consumers." *Powers of the Mind: The Reinvention of Liberal Learning* (University of Chicago Press, 2006), 4. John McKnight and Peter Block go even further: "The culture of the university is no longer a place for education; it is a terminal to pass through in order to get somewhere . . . It has replaced the creation of learning with the consumption of instruction." *The Abundant Community,* 61.

50. James B. Stewart, "New Metric for Colleges: Graduates' Salaries," *The New York Times,* September 13, 2013.

51. Fred Hirsch, *Social Limits to Growth* (Academic Press, 1976), 5. And Randall Collins argued more than thirty years ago that a "downturn in the national economy coinciding with a point of particularly obvious overinflation of the costs of cultural prestige may be the formula for an anticultural revolution." *The Credential Society: An Historical Sociology of Education and Stratification* (Academic Press, 1979), 71.

52. For a useful discussion of such socialization, see Susan K. Gardner and Pilar Mendoza, eds., *On Becoming a Scholar: Socialization and Development in Doctoral Education* (Stylus, 2010), p. xiv.

53. Damrosch, *We Scholars,* 148.

54. Elizabeth Minnich/Brown email 7/5/13.

55. Thomas J. Haskell, *Objectivity Is Not Neutrality: Explanatory Schemes in History* (Johns Hopkins University Press, 2000), 7.

56. Charles E. Lindblom, *Inquiry and Change: The Troubled Attempt to Understand and Shape Society* (Yale University Press, 1990), 199.

57. Melissa McDaniels, "Doctoral Socialization for Teaching Roles," in *On Becoming a Scholar,* Gardner and Mendoza, eds., 32.

58. Mary Ann Murphy/Brown email 5/30/13.

59. Bernie Ronan/Brown email 2/28/13.

60. David Cooper/Brown email 3/18/13. I am reminded of Stuart Firestein's observation while leaning on W. B. Yeats: "Education is not the filling of a pail, but the lighting of a fire." Stuart Firestein, *Ignorance: How It Drives Science* (Oxford University Press, 2012), 176.

61. David Cooper/Brown email 3/18/13.

62. Clifford Geertz, *Local Knowledge: Further Essays in Interpretive Anthropology* (Basic Books, 1983), 155.

63. Ibid.,173.

64. Ibid., 187.

65. Wilensky, "The Professionalization of Everyone?" 146–147.

Chapter 2

1. Laurence Veysey, *The Emergence of the American University* (University of Chicago Press, 1965), 337–38.

2. John Dewey, *The Quest for Certainty* (Paragon Books, 1979), 312–13.

3. Thomas Sowell, *Knowledge and Decisions* (Basic Books, 1980), 10.

4. Adam Smith, *The Wealth of Nations* (Penguin Books, 1977), 112.

5. Susan K. Gardner and Pilar Mendoza, eds., *On Becoming A Scholar: Socialization and Development in Doctoral Education* (Stylus, 2010), 11, 17.

6. Alfred North Whitehead, *Science and the Modern World* (Free Press, 1967), 197.

7. Donald A. Schon, *The Reflective Practitioner: How Professionals Think in Action* (Basic Books, 1983), 345.

8. Talcott Parsons, "The Academic System: A Sociologist's View," *Public Interest* 13 (Fall 1968): 182.

9. John J. Corson, *The Governance of Colleges and Universities* (McGraw-Hill, 1975), 78.

10. Chris Golde, "Entering Different Worlds: Socialization Into Disciplinary Communities," in Gardner and Mendoza, *On Becoming a Scholar*, 83.

11. Alex Bentley, Mark Earls, and Michael J. O'Brien, *I'll Have What She's Having: Mapping Social Behavior* (MIT Press, 2011), p. xi.

12. Dawn Shinew and Tami Moore, "Exploring Epistemological Diversity in a Doctoral Seminar," in Gardner and Mendoza, *On Becoming a Scholar*, 260–61.

13. John Dewey, *Experience and Education* (Collier Books, 1938), 19.

14. John Dewey, *The Quest for Certainty* (Paragon, 1979), 252.

15. Barry Schwartz, *The Battle for Human Nature: Science, Morality and Modern Life* (W. W. Norton, 1986), 325.

16. Mary Zey, *Rational Choice Theory and Organizational Theory: A* Critique (Sage Publications, 1997), 24.

17. Philip Tetlock, *Expert Political Judgment: How Good Is It? How Can We Know?* (Princeton University Press, 2005), 162.

18. Michael Schrage, *Serious Play: How the World's Best Companies Simulate to Innovate* (Harvard Business School Press, 2000), 66.

19. Ibid., 70.

20. Martin Carcasson/Brown email 3/18/13.

21. Cooper/Brown email 3/18/13.

22. KerryAnn O'Meara/Brown email 3/5/13.

23. Doherty/Brown email 3/11/13.
24. Minnich/Brown email 7/5/13.
25. Ibid.
26. Jacqueline Stevens, "Political Scientists are Lousy Forecasters," *The New York Times*, June 23, 2012.
27. Nate Silver, *The Signal and the Noise: Why So Many Predictions Fail—But Some Don't* (Penguin Press, 2012), 177
28. Edward B. Burger and Michael Starbird, *Coincidences, Chaos, and All That Math Jazz* (W.W. Norton, 2005), 41.
29. Silver, *The Signal and the Noise*, 183.
30. Ibid., 212.
31. Ibid., 33.
32. Ibid., 183.
33. Tetlock, *Expert Political Judgment*, 52–53.
34. Scott Page, *The Difference: How the Power of Diversity Creates Better Groups, Firms, Schools, and Societies* (Princeton University Press, 2007), 101.
35. Bent Flyvbjerg, *Making Social Science Matter: Why Social Inquiry Fails and How It Can Succeed Again* (Cambridge University Press, 2001), 73.
36. Silver, *The Signal and the Noise*, 14.
37. James C. Scott, *Seeing Like a State: How Certain Schemes to Improve the Human Condition Have Failed* (Yale University Press, 1998), 294.
38. Schrage, *Serious Play*, 70.
39. Tetlock, *Expert Political Judgment*, 63.
40. Foreword, in Roberta Wohlstetter, *Pearl Harbor: Warning and Decision* (Stanford University Press, 1962), p. vii.
41. Silver, *The Signal and the Noise*, 64.
42. Tetlock, *Expert Political Judgment*, 162.
43. Schrage, *Serious Play*, 56, 117.
44. Ibid., 120.
45. Melanie Mitchell, *Complexity: A Guided Tour* (Oxford University Press, 2009), 300.
46. M. Mitchell Waldrop, *Complexity: The Emerging Science at the Edge of Order and Chaos* (Simon & Schuster, 1992), 142.
47. Don K. Price, *The Scientific Estate* (Belknap Press, 1965), 195–96.
48. Randall Collins, *The Credential Society*, 54, 90.
49. Ivan Illich, *Disabling Professions* (Marion Boyars, 1978), 24.
50. John McKnight, "Professionalized Service and Disabling Help," in Illich, *Disabling Professions*, 85.
51. Lionel Trilling, *Beyond Culture: Essays on Literature and Learning* (Harcourt Brace, 1979), 9.
52. Walker Percy, *The Message in the Bottle*, 54.

53. Sean Wilentz, *The Rise of Democracy*, 21.

54. Robert H. Wiebe, *Self-Rule: A Cultural History of American Democracy* (University of Chicago Press, 1995), 39.

55. Walter Lippmann, *Public Opinion* (Free Press, 1965), 171.

56. Wiebe, *Self-Rule*, 134, 180.

57. Robert B. Westbrook, *John Dewey and American Democracy* (Cornell University Press, 1991), 281–82.

58. Dewey quoted in Dzur, *Democratic Professionalism*, 119.

59. James A. Morone, *The Democratic Wish: Popular Participation and the Limits of American Government* (Yale University Press, 1998), 115.

60. Ibid., 98.

61. Albert Dzur takes note of William Sullivan's study of professionalism, which claims that the technocratic model professionalism that has advanced has "real costs that have come to public awareness in recent years: the costs of failed social policies, instrumental, self-interested professional practices, and harmful social stratification." *Democratic Professionalism*, 124.

62. Harry Boyte, "Public Work: Civic Populism Versus Technocracy in Higher Education," in *Agent of Democracy: Higher Education and the HEX Journey*, ed. David W. Brown and Deborah Witte (Kettering Foundation, 2008), 83.

63. Michael J. Sandel, *Democracy's Discontent: America in Search of a Public Philosophy* (Belknap Press of the Harvard University Press, 1996), 349.

64. Thomas Bender, "Historians in Public," http://publicsphere.ssrc.org/bender-historians-in-public/, posted 9/5/11.

65. David Warfield Brown, *The Real Change-Makers: Why Government Is Not the Problem Or the Solution* (Praeger, 2012), 2.

66. Christopher Lasch, *The Revolt of the Elites and the Betrayal of Democracy* (W.W. Norton, 1996), 41.

67. Christopher Hayes, *The Twilight of the Elites*, 113.

68. Charles E. Lindblom and David K. Cohen, *Usable Knowledge: Social Science and Social Problem Solving* (Yale University Press, 1979), 15.

69. Daniel J. Boorstin, *Democracy and Its Discontents: Reflections on Everyday America* (Random House, 1974), 121.

70. Edith Hamilton, *The Greek Way to Civilization* (Mentor Books, 1960), 14.

71. Frederick Hayek, *The Constitution of Liberty* (University of Chicago Press, Phoenix edition, 1978), 38.

72. Steven Brint, *In an Age of Experts*, 15.

73. Ibid., 18.

74. Jurgen Habermas, *Theory and Practice* (Beacon Press 1974), 256.

75. David Riesman, "Some Observations on Community Plans and Utopia," *Yale Law Journal* 57, 2 (December, 1947: 178–180. It reminds me of William Barrett's warning that he could "imagine a technical society of the future

that had conquered its material problems but was afflicted with a loss of meaning that its own technical thinking left it unable to grasp." *The Illusions of Technique* (Anchor Books, 1979), p. xx.

76. Richard Hofstadter, *Anti-Intellectualism in American Life* (Vintage Books, 1963), 46.

77. Thomas Bender, *Intellect and Public Life* (Johns Hopkins University Press, 1993), 10.

78. Chris Hayes argues that "extreme inequity" separates experts from lay publics and leads to the "paradoxical outcome" that "produces a worse caliber of elites." *Twilight of the Elites*, 155.

79. Alfred North Whitehead said a problem for education is "how to produce the expert without the loss of the essential virtues of the amateur." *The Aims of Education*, 13.

80. Abraham Maslow, *The Psychology of Science* (Harper & Row, 1966), 151.

81. Ralph Waldo Emerson, "The American Scholar," *The American Tradition of Literature* (W.W. Norton, 1961), 1040.

82. Alfred North Whitehead, *Science and the Modern World*, 197.

83. Lewis Thomas, "The Art of Teaching Science," *The New York Times Magazine* (March 14, 1982), 93.

84. Michael Polanyi explained: "The process of examining any topic is both an exploration of the topic, and an exegesis of our fundamental beliefs in the light of which we approach it; a dialectical combination of exploration and exegesis." *Personal Knowledge: Towards a Post-Critical Philosophy* (University of Chicago Press, 1962), 267.

Chapter 3

1. Harold L. Wilensky, "The Professionalization of Everyone?" *The American Journal of Sociology* LXX, 2 (September, 1964): 140.

2. David W. Brown, "Daring to be Unprofessional" *Higher Education Exchange* (1997): 11.

3. Derek W. M. Barker and David W. Brown, eds., *A Different Kind of Politics: Readings on the Role of Higher Education in Democracy* (Kettering Foundation Press, 2009), 53.

4. Steven J. Harper, *The Lawyer Bubble: A Profession in Crisis* (Basic Books, 2013), p. xvi.

5. Ibid., 77.

6. Ibid., 86. According to Harper, there is "little incentive" for senior partners to mentor young associates when "there is no way for partners to bill that time" (p. 92). Harper should know, having practiced for thirty years at a leading firm in Chicago.

7. As Randall Collins points out: "The elite legal profession thus organized itself through the cultural and political mobilization of the late nineteenth-century ethnic crisis." Collins goes on to note that in the twentieth century, the American Bar Association helped "to reassert upper-class and especially WASP control within the profession, and by extension, in politics as well." *The Credentialed Society*, 153.

8. Andrew Ross Sorkin, "Big Law Steps Into Uncertain Times" *The New York Times*, September 24, 2012.

9. Harper, *The Lawyer Bubble*, 100.

10. William S. Sullivan, *Work and Integrity*, 136, 134.

11. Steven Brint, *In an Age of Experts*, 9.

12. Brian Z. Tamanaha, *Failing Law Schools* (University of Chicago Press, 2012), pp. xii, 101, 109, 124.

13. Ibid., 139.

14. Harper, *The Lawyer Bubble*, 127.

15. Ethan Bronner, "Law Schools' Applications Fall as Costs Rise and Jobs are Cut," *The New York Times*, January 30, 2013.

16. Tamanaha, *Failing Law Schools*, 42.

17. David Segal, "What They Don't Teach Law Students: Lawyering" *The New York Times*, November 21, 2010.

18. Harper, *The Lawyer Bubble*, 46.

19. Ibid.

20. Tamanaha, *Failing Law Schools*, 55.

21. Thomas Bender, *Intellect and Public Life*, 143.

22. Harper, *The Lawyer Bubble*, 162–3.

23. Dr. Susan Dorr Goold, a researcher in a study of more than twenty patient focus groups, quoted in Pauline W. Chen, "Getting Patients to Think about Costs" *The New York Times*, February 21, 2013.

24. "When to Say 'Whoa!' to Your Doctor," *Consumer Reports* (June 12, 2012): 3.

25. Robert Pear, "Doctors Who Profit from Radiation Prescribe It More Often, Study Finds," *The New York Times*, August 18, 2013.

26. Roni Caryn Rabin, "Doctor Panels Recommend Fewer Tests for Patients," *The New York Times*, April 4, 2012.

27. Peter B. Bach, "The Trouble with Doctor Knows Best," *The New York Times*, June 4, 2012.

28. Randall Watt/Brown email 6/22/13.

29. Roni Caryn Rabin, "Doctors' Lucrative Industry Ties," *The New York Times*, May 13, 2013.

30. Reed Abelson, Julie Cresswell, and Griffin J. Palmer "Medicare Bills Rise as Records Turn Electronic," *The New York Times*, September 21, 2012.

31. William Hanson, *Smart Medicine: How the Changing Role of Doctors Will Revolutionize Health Care* (Palgrave Macmillan, 2011), 102.

32. Jessica Silver-Greenberg, "Patients Mired in Costly Credit from Doctors," *The New York Times*, October 14, 2013.

33. Jane E. Brody, "When Costly Medical Care Just Adds to the Pain," *The New York Times*, May 28, 2012.

34. Robert S. Kaplan and Michael E. Porter, "Why Medical Bills Are a Mystery," *The New York Times*, April 14, 2012.

35. Annie Lowery and Robert Pear, "Doctor Shortage Likely to Worsen with Health Law," *The New York Times*, July 28, 2012.

36. H. Gilbert Welch, "Diagnosis: Insufficient Outrage," *The New York Times*, July 4, 2013.

37. Joshua T. Cohen, Peter J. Neumann, and Milton C. Weinstein, "Does Preventive Care Save Money?" *New England Journal of Medicine* (February 14, 2008): 661.

38. Michael Pollan, "Big Food v. Big Insurance," *The New York Times*, September 10, 2009.

39. Roni Caryn Rabin, "Obese Americans Spend Far More on Health Care," *The New York Times*, July 28, 2009.

40. Association of Schools of Public Health, "What Is Public Health?" www.whatispublichealth.org/impact/achievements.html.

41. Sandeep Jauhar, "Out of Camelot, Knights in White Coats Lose Their Way," *The New York Times,* January, 31, 2011.

42. "In Bakersfield, California, a Mexican strawberry picker with an income of $14,000 and no English was lent every penny he needed to buy a house for $724,000." *The Big Short: Inside the Doomsday Machine* (W.W. Norton, 2010), 23–24, 97.

43. Nate Silver, *The Signal and the Noise*, 20.

44. Floyd Norris, "In Actions, S & P Risked Andersen's Fate," *The New York Times*, February 7, 2013. Norris also noted that more recently the public Accounting Oversight Board reported that Ernst & Young, one of the "Big Four" accounting firms, had "identified a fraud risk" in nine audits, but the firm had relied on figures provided by corporate executives without further evaluation. Ernst had accepted management assumptions without further challenge. "Regulator Cites Flaws in Ernst & Young's Audit Procedures," *The New York Times*, May 23, 2013.

45. For a down-to-earth explanation of the financial swoon, see Chicago Public Media and Ira Glass, *This American Life*, "The Great Pool of Money" www.thisamericanlife.org/radio-archives/episode/355/transcript.

46. Andrew Ross Sorkin, "On Wall Street, a Culture of Greed Won't Let Go," *The New York Times,* July 15, 2013.

47. Ibid.

48. Jonathan R. Macey, *The Death of Corporate Reputation: How Integrity Has Been Destroyed on Wall Street* (Financial Times Press, 2013), 12.

49. Ibid., 11.

50. I recall the struggle at Yale's School of Management (SOM), where I taught for ten years. During my last year at SOM before I assumed the presidency of a small liberal arts college in Illinois, there were major changes underway in SOM's management, staffing, and curriculum. Up until that time, SOM had offered what many students, and some faculty, considered a welcome alternative to the traditional business school curriculum. SOM was attracting students, in part, because of its interdisciplinary program, which taught public as well as private-sector management and stressed "people skills" through "experiential workshops." With a new dean, however, who replaced six non-tenured organizational development/organizational behavior faculty, Benno Schmidt, Yale's new president, sought to reposition SOM in the mainstream of business schools by seeking out more "quantitative theoreticians." Schmidt did not last long at Yale, but unfortunately, the changes he imposed did.

51. Macey, *The Death of Corporate Reputation,* 266–68.

52. Kelly Ward, "Doctoral Student Socialization for Service," in *On Becoming a Scholar: Socialization and Development in Doctoral Education,* ed. Susan K. Gardner and Pilar Mendoza (Stylus Publishing, 2010), 62, 64.

53. Cooper/Brown email 3/18/13.

54. Michael Oakeshott, *The Voice of Liberal Learning: Michael Oakeshott on Education,* ed. Timothy Fuller (Yale University Press, 1989), 96.

55. According to Randall Collins, a profession "has exclusive power, usually backed up by the state, to train new members and admit them to practice. It practices its specialty according to its own standards without outside interference. It reserves the right to judge its own members' performance, and resists incursions of lay opinion . . . It has a code of ethics, claiming to dedicate its work to the service of humanity, pledging disinterested and competent performance, and condemning commercialism and careerism." *The Credential Society,* 132.

56. Cooper/Brown email 3/18/13.

57. Minnich/Brown email 7/5/13.

58. Doherty/Brown email 3/10/13.

59. David W. Brown, "Professional Virtue: A Dangerous Kind of Humbug," *Change* (November/December, 1985): 46.

60. Jacques Barzun, "The Professions Under Siege," *Harper's,* (October, 1978): 65–66.

61. With tongue in cheek, Veysey observes that "magicians who lack self-confidence, from whatever motive, invite disrespect from onlookers." *The Emergence of the American University* (University of Chicago Press, 1965), 355.
62. Ralph Waldo Emerson, "The American Scholar," 75.
63. Ronan/Brown email 2/28/13.
64. John McKnight, *Disabling Professions* (Marion Boyers, 1978), 74.
65. Samuel Haber, *Quest for Authority and Honor*, p. xii.

Chapter 4

1. David Weinberger, *Everything Is Miscellaneous: The Power of the New Digital Disorder* (Times Books, Henry Holt and Company, 2007), 230.
2. Ibid.,147.
3. Ibid., 133.
4. Bentley et al., *I'll Have What She's Having*, p. xii.
5. Louis Menand, *The Metaphysical Club: A Story of Ideas in America* (Farrar, Straus and Giroux, 2001), p. xi
6. Albert Dzur, *Democratic Professionalism*, 117.
7. Kenneth Bruffee, *Collaborative Learning: Higher Education, Interdependence and the Authority of Knowledge* (Johns Hopkins University Press, 1993), 8.
8. Steven Johnson, *Emergence: The Connected Lives of Ants, Brains, Cities, and Software* (Scribner, 2001), 234.
9. Bruffee, 71, 98.
10. Ibid., 2.
11. It was Kuhn who saw that textbooks hide the processes from which such knowledge emerges. *The Structure of Scientific Revolutions*, 2d ed. (University of Chicago Press,, 1970), 140, 210).
12. David Weinberger, *Too Big To Know: Rethinking Knowledge Now That the Facts Aren't the Facts, Experts Are Everywhere, and the Smartest Person in the Room Is the Room* (Basic Books, 2011), 151.
13. James Surowiecki, *The Wisdom of Crowds: Why the Many Are Smarter Than the Few and How Collective Wisdom Shapes Business, Economies, Societies, and Nations* (Doubleday, 2004), 161.
14. Thomas Lin, "Cracking Open the Scientific Process," *The New York Times*, January 16, 2012.
15. Surowiecki, *The Wisdom of Crowds*, 30.
16. Page also sees cognitive diversity promoting new "norms of sharing and diversity." *The Difference: The Power of Diversity Creates Better Groups, Firms, Schools, and Societies* (Princeton University Press, 2007), pp. xviii, 17–18.
17. Paul Markham and Eric Bain-Selbo at Western Kentucky University "Did I Teach Them That? The Implicit Power of Democratic Education,"

October 18, 2012, ejournal.missouristate.edu/2012/09/did-I-teach-them-that-the-implicit-power-of-democratic-education.

18. Parker J. Palmer, *Healing the Heart of Democracy: The Courage to Create a Politics Worthy of the Human Spirit* (Jossey-Bass, 2011), 133. Richard Sennett adds that "As social animals we are capable of cooperation more deeply than the existing social order envisions." *Together: The Rituals, Pleasures and Politics of Cooperation* (Yale University Press, 2012), 280.

19. William G. Bowen, *Higher Education in the Digital Age* (Princeton University Press, 2013), 68.

20. William M. Sullivan, *Work and Integrity: The Crisis and Promise of Professionalism in America* (HarperCollins, 1995), 220.

21. David W. Brown, *When Strangers Cooperate: Using Social Conventions to Govern Ourselves* (Free Press, 1995), 11.

22. *Zagat New York City Restaurants 2010* (Zagat Survey, LLC, 2009), 5.

23. McKnight and Block, *The Abundant Community*, 14.

24. Michael Schrage, *Serious Play*, 88.

25. Tom Standage, "Social Networking in the 1600s" *The New York Times,* June 22, 2013.

26. Michael Gibbons, Camille Limoges, Helga Nowotny, Simon Schwartzman, Peter Scott, and Martin Trow, *The New Production of Knowledge: The Dynamics of Science and Research in Contemporary Societies* (Sage Publications, 1994), 14.

27. Ibid., 3, 6.

28. Ibid., 8–10.

29. Graff, *Beyond the Culture Wars*, 111. William Sullivan thinks that the power of "positivism" as "a theory of science" is still substantial "as a kind of ideology." Sullivan sees that such "positivist dogma" in higher education "must be confronted by anyone who seeks to reshape professional knowledge as well as the way professional life is organized" *Work and Integrity*, 166.

30. William Bowen devoted his 2012 Tanner Lectures at Stanford to such a subject: "I too am convinced that online learning *could be* truly transformative." However, he went on to explain: "There is something of an inherent conflict, or at least a tension, between, on the one hand, the structure of MOOC offerings [massive open online courses], which are designed largely by renowned and high-visibility professors at leading universities and which are generally provided worldwide on an 'as is' basis and, on the other hand, the need for at least some campus-specific customization." *Higher Education in the Digital Age*, 59. In the same lectures, Andrew Delbanco of Columbia University added: "How can we apply traditional measures such as retention or completion rates to these new educational 'delivery systems'? And if we can't, how can we assess their educational value alongside their revenue-producing value?" (p. 140).

31. Joichi Ito, "In an Open Source Society, Innovating by the Seat of Your Pants," *The New York Times*, December 5, 2011.

32. Lawrence A. Cremin, *Popular Education and Its Discontents* (Harper & Row, 1989), 57.

33. David Weinberger, *Too Big To Know*, p. xiii.

34. Ibid., 67

35. Ibid., 113.

36. Nicholas Carr, *The Shallows: What the Internet Is Doing to Our Brains* (W. W. Norton, 2010), 112, 114.

37. Ibid., 120.

38. Andrew Keen, *The Cult of the Amateur: How Today's Internet is Killing Our Culture* (Doubleday/Currency, 2007), 44.

39. Ibid., 56.

40. Susan Cain, "The Rise of Groupthink," *The New York Times*, January 13, 2012. Cain is the author of *Quiet: The Power of Introverts in a World That Can't Stop Talking* (Crown Publishers, 2012).

41. Mathew Hindman, *The Myth of Digital Democracy* (Princeton University Press, 2010), 13.

42. Howard Rheingold, *Smart Mobs: The Next Social Revolution* (Basic Books, 2002), 60.

43. Eric S. Raymond, *The Cathedral and the Bazaar: Musings on Linux and Open Source by an Accidental Revolutionary* (O'Reilly, 2001), 16. As co-editor of the Kettering Foundation's *Higher Education Exchange*, I once compared our conversation with educators in the pages of HEX as a distant cousin to the open source process. Since those in academe have no property software code to run the higher education system, we wanted to offer to them the "access and opportunities to improve what they find." "Talking the Walk: Making Sense of HEX (1994–2004)," *Higher Education Exchange* (2004), 5.

44. Steven Weber, *The Success of Open Source* (Harvard University Press, 2004), 228.

45. Jedediah Purdy, *The Meaning of Property*, 155.

46. Clay Shirky, *Cognitive Surplus: Creativity and Generosity in a Connected Age* (Penguin Press, 2010), 155.

47. Ibid., 157–158

48. J. Walker Smith and Ann Clurman, *Generation Ageless: How Baby Boomers are Changing the Way We Live Today . . . and They're Just Getting Started* (Harper-Collins, 2007), 65–66.

49. William C. Taylor, "Here's an Idea: Let Everyone Have Ideas," *The New York Times*, March 26, 2013.

50. Raymond, *The Cathedral and the Bazaar*, 81.

51. Daren C. Brabham, *Crowdsourcing* (MIT Press, 2013), 44.

52. Ibid., p. xix.
53. Ibid., 73.
54. Chris Anderson, *The Long Tail: Why the Future of Business is Selling Less of More* (Hyperion, 2006), 68, 73, 184.
55. Shirky, *Cognitive Surplus*, 186.
56. Weinberger, *Everything is Miscellaneous*, 102.
57. O'Meara/Brown email 5/30/13. However, another professor told me: "It is important to maintain a distinction between knowledge and data. Knowledge is systemic and about verification and justification, while data is about management and storage." Murphy/Brown email 5/30/13.
58. Carcasson/Brown email 3/18/13.
59. Kenneth Bruffee, *Collaborative Learning*, 36.
60. Ibid., 5–6.
61. Ibid., 192
62. Parker Palmer, *The Courage to Teach: Exploring the Inner Landscape of a Teacher's Life* (Jossey-Bass, 1998), 51. In another of his writings, Palmer says: "Too many students spend long hours in classrooms where they are mere audience to a teacher's performance. They become passive recipients of expert knowledge rather than active participants in a process of inquiry, discovery, and co-creation." *Healing the Heart of Democracy: The Courage to Create a Politics Worthy of the Human Spirit* (Jossey-Bass, 2011), 133.
63. Charles W. Anderson, *Prescribing the Life of the Mind: An Essay on the Purpose of the University, the Aims of Liberal Education, the Competence of Citizens, and the Cultivation of Practical Reason* (University of Wisconsin Press, 1993), 87.
64. Palmer, *Healing the Heart of Democracy*, 132–133.
65. Delbanco, *College: What It Was, Is, and Should Be*, 58.
66. Stanley Fish, "Why We Built the Ivory Tower" *The New York Times*, May 21, 2004.
67. David Brooks, "The Relationship School," *The New York Times*, March 22, 2012.
68. Ibid.
69. www.exeter/admissions/109_1220_11688.aspx (6/12/13).
70. Thomas Hassan/Brown email 7/1/13.
71. Wick Sloane/Brown email 6/6/13.
72. Richard Schubart/Brown email 8/27/13. When I asked Schubart what he thought one of the greater weaknesses of the Harkness method, he told me: "It requires considerable preparation in advance for the conversation or inquiry to be meaningful; otherwise [it] can lead to sophistry."
73. Bruffee, *Collaborative Learning*, 66.
74. Schubart/Brown email 8/27/13
75. James Holtz '64, exeter.edu/exeter_bulletin/12984_13037.aspx (8/28/13).
76. Isaiah Brown/Brown email 6/12/13.

77. Ibid.
78. Anna Brown/Brown email 7/14/13.
79. Hassan/Brown email 7/1/13.
80. Thomas Hassan, "Exeter's Immediate Priorities," www.exeter.edu/documents/Exeter_Immediate_Priorities_1_20_12pdf, 3.
81. Isaiah Brown/Brown email 6/12/13.
82. Ibid.
83. Schubart/Brown email 8/27/13.
84. Anna Brown/Brown email 7/1/4/13.
85. Schubart/Brown email 8/27/13.
86. Ibid.
87. Benson et al., *Dewey's Dream*, 85.
88. Polanyi and Prosch, *Meaning*, 3.
89. Peter L. Berger and Thomas Luckman, *The Social Construction of Reality* (Random House, 1966), 23.
90. Malcolm Gladwell, *Outliers: The Story of Success* (Little, Brown, 2008), 102.
91. Donald A. Schon, *Educating the Reflective Practitioner* (Jossey-Bass, 1987), 37–38. For purposes of my discussion here I would exclude what some might call the "social learning" of students—such as surfing the Internet and a shared social life with friends both on campus and off. Richard Arum and Joseph Roksa, *Academically Adrift: Limited Learning on College Campuses* (University of Chicago Press, 2011), 62.
92. Charles E. Lindblom, *Inquiry and Change: The Troubled Attempt to Understand and Shape Society* (Yale University Press and Russell Sage Foundation, 1990), 217.
93. Charles E. Lindblom and David K. Cohen, *Usable Knowledge: Social Science and Social Problem Solving* (Yale University Press, 1979), 19.
94. Ibid.
95. Ibid., 10.
96. Lawrence A. Cremin, *American Education: The Colonial Experience* (Harper & Row, 1970), 192–193, 266.
97. Lawrence A. Cremin, *American Education: The Metropolitan Experience, 1876–1980* (Harper & Row, 1988), 652.
98. David Mathews, *The Ecology of Democracy: Finding Ways to Have a Stronger Hand in Shaping Our Future* (Kettering Foundation Press, 2014), 109.

Chapter 5

1. R. B. Bernstein, *Thomas Jefferson* (Oxford University Press, 2003), 75–76.
2. E. J. Dionne, Jr., *Our Divided Political Heart: The Battle for the American Idea in an Age of Discontent* (Bloomsbury, 2012), 179.

3. Albert W. Dzur, *Democratic Professionalism: Citizen Participation and the Reconstruction of Professional Ethics, Identity, and Practice* (Pennsylvania State University Press, 2008), 75, 101.

4. Bill Schambra quoted in Cynthia Gibson, *Citizens at the Center* (Case Foundation, 2006), 23.

5. John L. McKnight, "Regenerating Community" (*Social Policy*, Winter 1987), 54–57, 58. David Mathews in *The Ecology of Democracy*, 82, 84. Mathews thinks of expert knowledge, which is "technical and scarce," as "necessary" but "not sufficient to produce sound judgments"—judgments that also depend on citizen knowledge that is "normative and common" growing out of everyday experience.

6. Matt Leighninger, *The Next Form of Democracy: How Expert Rule Is Giving Way to Shared Governance . . . and Why Politics Will Never Be the Same* (Vanderbilt University Press, 2006), 67.

7. Matt Leighninger, "Citizen-Centered Democracy: An Interview with Matt Leighninger" *Higher Education Exchange,* 2009, 14, 15. Richard Sennett notes: "Mutual support is built into the genes of all social animals, they cooperate to accomplish what they can't do alone." *Together: The Rituals, Pleasures and Politics of Cooperation* (Yale University Press, 2012), 5.

8. Matt Leighninger, "Mapping Deliberative Civic Engagement: Pictures from a (R)evolution," in *Democracy in Motion: Evaluating the Practice and Impact of Deliberative Civic Engagement,* ed. Tina Nabatchi, John Gastil, G. Michael Weiksner, and Matt Leighninger (Oxford University Press, 2012), 20.

9. Derek W. M. Barker, Noelle McAfee, and David W. McIver, eds., *Democratizing Deliberation: A Political Theory Anthology* (Kettering Foundation Press, 2012), 9.

10. David Mathews, *The Ecology of Democracy*, 55.

11. Leighninger, "Mapping Deliberative Civic Engagement," 36. David Mathews has credited such deliberative experience for encouraging citizens that if they "can claim responsibility and act in one community, they can become the 'solution' they are looking for in other communities." *Politics for People: Finding a Responsible Public Voice* (University of Illinois Press, 1994), 195.

12. As David Mathews notes: "Unfortunately, many engagement efforts start where the organizers start—with *their* names for issues, with *their* framework for decision-making, and with *their* answers to problems at hand." *The Ecology of Democracy*, 94.

13. John Dewey, *The Public and Its Problems* (Swallow Press, 1988), 151. Philosophy professor, Noelle McAfee, put it succinctly: "If we are to make and remake our world democratically, we all need to have an equal, and yet still distinct and special, role in that project." "Public Scholarship, or How to

Assist in the Autopoiesis of Political Communities," *Higher Education Exchange* (2009): 13.

14. James C. Scott, *Seeing Like a State*, 317.

15. Borrowing an observation of Frank Fischer in *Citizens, Experts, and the Environment*, Albert Dzur argues: "Laypeople" are "more particularistic, more attentive to historical dimensions, and more relationship and person oriented than expert knowledge." Dzur, *Democratic Professionalism*, 128–29.

16. From his own experience in public administration, Ronan thinks that "there are few places with true deliberation . . . being pursued to engage the public . . . but the topic has grown in salience within the field." Ronan/Brown email 2/28/13.

17. Ibid.

18. Donald Schon, *The Reflective Practitioner*, 346.

19. Ibid., 61.

20. Ibid., 300.

21. Thomas Bender, *Intellect and Public Life*, 137.

22. Ibid., 10.

23. Minnich/Brown email 7/5/13.

24. Matt Miller argues: "the dumbest questions are almost always the smartest questions because they get at the fundamentals." *The Tyranny of Dead Ideas: Revolutionary Thinking for a New Age of Prosperity* (Henry Holt, 2010), 237.

25. David W. Brown, *Organization Smarts: Portable Skills for Professionals Who Want to Get Ahead* (AMACOM, 2002), 152.

26. Stuart Firestein, *Ignorance* (Oxford University Press, 2012), 17, 82.

27. Ibid., 10, 11, 16.

28. Bent Flyvbjerg has urged the social sciences to become "an activity done in public for the public, sometimes to clarify, sometimes to intervene, sometimes to generate new perspectives . . . in short, arrive at a social science that matters." *Making Social Science Matter*, 166.

29. Brown, *Organization Smarts*, 160.

30. Bender, *Intellect and Public Life*, 145. In discussing this and other matters with Professor Bender, we both recalled leaving our university offices to join the bewildered crowds of New Yorkers drawn to Union Square in the immediate aftermath of 9/11. It was a place, among many in the city, when both public thinking and public grieving were dramatically evident as strangers sought strangers to share their thoughts and feelings.

31. Doherty/Brown email 3/10/13.

32. Sheryl Gay Stolberg, "You Want Compromise? Sure You Do," *The New York Times,* August 18, 2011.

33. Michael J. Sandel, *What Money Can't Buy: The Moral Limits of Markets* (Farrar, Straus and Giroux, 2012), 202. Sandel cites an example in his

chapter "Jumping the Queue," of allowing money to buy its way to the head of a line with the equality of "first come, first served" thus being seriously compromised.

34. David Warfield Brown, *The Real Change-Makers*, 41.
35. Minnich/Brown email 7/5/13.
36. Sara M. Evans and Harry C. Boyte, *Free Spaces: The Sources of Democratic Change in America* (Harper & Row, 1986), 188.
37. Ibid., 192.
38. David W. Brown, *When Strangers Cooperate*, 80.
39. Harry C. Boyte, "Public Work," 94.
40. There is a National Coalition for Dialogue and Deliberation ("NCDD") that might share its network and resources with those who undertake a potluck deliberation, if some follow-through were pursued beyond the deliberation itself.
41. Barker and Brown, *A Different Kind of Politics*, 54. In his study of "democratic professionalism," Dzur cited Tocqueville, who saw America's jury system as a form of "task sharing" in which the "independent, self-confident American [was] socialized in orderly habits of formal decision making by taking part in formal discussion." *Democratic Professionalism*, 109.
42. Lynn M. Sanders, "Against Deliberation," *Political Theory* 25 (1997), 366–67.
43. Randolph N. Jonakait, *The American Jury System* (Yale University Press, 2003), 44, 47.
44. Nancy Thomas and Peter Levine, "Deliberative Democracy and Higher Education: Higher Education's Democratic Mission," in *To Serve a Larger Purpose: Engagement for Democracy and the Transformation of Higher Education,* ed. John Saltmarsh and Mathew Hartley (Temple University Press, 2011), 159.
45. Albert W. Dzur, *Punishment, Participatory Democracy and the Jury* (Oxford University Press, 2012), 57. Andrew Guthrie Ferguson points out that although the U.S. Constitution firmly established the place of juries to deliberate over how the law should be applied, local town meetings, community associations, and churches were also "designed spaces to practice deliberation." *Why Jury Duty Matters: A Citizen's Guide to Constitutional Action* (New York University Press, 2013), 108.
46. John Saltmarsh and Mathew Hartley, "Conclusion: Creating the Democratically Engaged University—Possibilities for Constructive Action," *"To Serve a Larger Purpose": Engagement for Democracy and the Transformation of Higher Education* (Temple University Press, 2011), 294, 296.
47. Gerald Graff, *Beyond the Culture Wars: How Teaching the Conflicts Can Revitalize American Education* (W. W. Norton, 1992), 146.
48. Saltmarsh and Hartley, *To Serve a Larger Purpose*, 298.

49. O'Meara/Brown email 3/15/13.
50. Minnich/Brown email 7/5/13.
51. Parker Palmer, *Healing the Heart of Democracy*, 34.
52. Saltmarsh and Hartley, *To Serve a Larger Purpose*, 290.
53. Dan W. Butin and Scott Seider, eds., *The Engaged Campus: Certificates, Minors, and Majors as the New Community Engagement* (Palgrave Macmillan, 2012), 5, 6.
54. Ibid., 7, 8.
55. Martin Carcasson, "Facilitating Community Democracy from Campus: Centers, Faculty, and Students as Key Resources of Passionate Impartiality," *Higher Education Exchange* (2010): 24.
56. Carcasson/Brown email 3/18/13.
57. Acquiring the skills for deliberation does not always require going off-campus. Obviously, such skills already have a place in classroom work. I asked David Cooper, an emeritus professor of writing, rhetoric, and American cultures how the priority of developing 'critical thinking' in higher education has been reconciled with the important skills of deliberation. Cooper thought this was "an extremely important question," and told me that in "the fields of Composition and Rhetoric, theories lumped together under the banner of 'critical pedagogy' are dominant. I see deliberative skills of democracy torqued in tension with critical pedagogy. For me, the rhetorical goals of deliberation are entirely consistent with durable critical thinking skills. The ideological climate 'problematizes' that linkage." Cooper/Brown email 3/18/13.
58. Douglas Challenger and Joni Doherty, "Living in the Lap of an Immense Intelligence: Lessons on Public Scholarship from the Field" *Higher Education Exchange* (2002): 60.
59. Douglas Challenger: "The New England Center for Civic Life: A Decade of Making a Difference," in *Agent of Democracy: Higher Education and the HEX Journey*, ed. David W. Brown and Deborah Witte (Kettering Foundation Press, 2008), 195.
60. Doherty/Brown email 3/10/13.
61. Barker and Brown, *A Different Kind of Politics*, 33–34.
62. Ibid.

Chapter 6

1. John McKnight, *The Careless Society: Community and Its Counterfeits* (Basic Books, 1995), 170.
2. McKnight and Block, *The Abundant Community*, 36.
3. Ibid., 40.

4. Gerald Graff, *Clueless in Academe: How Schooling Obscures the Life of the Mind* (Yale University Press, 2003), 228–229, 231. There are exceptions. John Brereton, an English professor at the University of Massachusetts at Boston, asks his students in First Year Composition to do a research paper "on something they know and are interested in." As a consequence, according to Brereton, "students . . . feel a real personal stake in their education, something you can't fake."

5. Eric S. Raymond, *The Cathedral and the Bazaar: Musings on Linux and Open Source by an Accidental Revolutionary* (O'Reilly, 2001), 38.

6. Harry Boyte, *Commonwealth: A Return to Citizen Politics* (Free Press, 1989), 231–32.

7. Robert Kingston and Peter Levine, "What is 'Public' About What Academics Do? An Exchange with Robert Kingston and Peter Levine," *Higher Education Exchange* (2004): 27.

8. Harry Boyte argues: "If we are interested in civic engagement and the empowerment of citizens . . . [they have] to be seen as a function of institutional cultures, not simply of individual proclivities." *Everyday Politics* (University of Pennsylvania Press, 2004), p. xi.

9. Pauline W. Chen, "Afraid to Speak Up at the Doctor's Office," *The New York Times*, May 31, 2012.

10. Thomas Jefferson, letter to William Charles Jarvis, September 28, 1820, *The Writings of Thomas Jefferson,* Library Edition issued under the auspices of the Thomas Jefferson Memorial Association of the United States, 1903, 278.

11. Evans and Boyte, *Free Spaces*, 17.

12. "Public Work: An Interview with Harry Boyte," *Higher Education Exchange* (2000): 45.

13. Ibid., 47

14. Barker and Brown, *A Different Kind of Politics*, 50.

15. "Public Work at Colgate: An Interview with Adam Weinberg," in *Agent of Democracy: Higher Education and the HEX Journey,* eds. David W. Brown and Deborah Witte (Kettering Foundation Press, 2008), 103–18.

16. Adam Weinberg, "Preparing a Generation to do Public Work," (Address to Ohio Campus Compact, August 7, 2013).

17. Mark Wilson and Nan Fairley, "Living Democracy: A Project for Students and Citizens" *Higher Education Exchange* (2012): 37.

18. David Mathews, *The Ecology of Democracy*, 151.

19. Ellison/Brown email 9/6/13.

20. Barker and Brown, *A Different Kind of Politics,* 71.

21. Ibid., 74.

22. "Changing Public Culture: An Interview with Marguerite S. Shaffer" *Higher Education Exchange* (2008): 24.

23. Ibid., 29, 30, 33.
24. Ellen M. Knutson and Dan A. Lewis, "Civic Engagement and Doctoral Education," *Higher Education Exchange* (2012): 49.
25. Ibid., 50, 52.
26. Ibid., 48.
27. Harry Boyte, "Public Work: Civic Populism Versus Technocracy in Higher Education," in Brown and Witte, *Agent of Democracy*, 80.
28. Boyte, "Public Work: An Interview with Harry Boyte," 48.
29. Boyte, "Civic Populism," 81.
30. Boyte, "Public Work" in *Agent of Democracy*, 94–95.
31. ACP 2/13/12 newsletter (boyte001@unm.edu).
32. "Higher Education and the American Commonwealth Partnership: An Interview with Harry Boyte," *Higher Education Exchange* (2012): 9, 10, 11.
33. Harry C. Boyte, "Reinventing Citizenship as Public Work," (Kettering Foundation, 2013), 28.
34. Peters is especially interested in how such scholarship can facilitate a shift to sustainable food systems. http://hort.cals.cornell.edu/people/scott-peters (2/16/14)
35. Jeremy Cohen, ed. "A Laboratory for Public Scholarship and Democracy: New Directions for Teaching and Learning" (*Jossey-Bass*, April 2006): 14.
36. Ellison/Brown email 9/6/13.
37. ImaginingAmerica.org/fg-item/scholarship-in-public-knowledge-creation-and tenure-policy-in-the-engaged-university/ (10/12/13).
38. Ellison Brown email 9/6/13.
39. Lawrence A. Cremin, *Traditions of American Education* (Basic Books, 1977), 78, 82, 84, 104, 177.
40. William S. Sullivan, *Work and Integrity: The Crisis and Promise of Professionalism in America* (Harper/Collins, 1995), 18, 75, 78.
41. Jean Bethke Elshtain, *Jane Addams and the Dream of American Democracy: A Life* (Basic Books, 2002), p. xxi.
42. Westbrook, *John Dewey and American Democracy*, 164.
43. Jane Addams quoted in Louise W. Knight, *Citizen: Jane Addams and the Struggle for Democracy* (University of Chicago Press, 2005), frontispiece.
44. Menand, *The Metaphysical Club*, 311–12.
45. David W. Brown, "The Journey of a Recovering Professional," *Higher Education Exchange* (2008): 10–11.
46. Murphy/Brown email 5/29/13.
47. Carol Gilligan, *In a Different Voice: Psychological Theory and Women's Development* (Harvard University Press, 1982), 159.
48. Allison Fine, *Momentum: Igniting Social Change in the Connected Age* (Jossey-Bass, 2006), 60.

49. "Engaged Faculty: An Interview with KerryAnn O'Meara," *Higher Education Exchange* (2011): 22.

50. Diana Meehan quoted in Sally Helgesen, *The Female Advantage: Women's Ways of Leadership* (Currency Doubleday, 1995), 35. Diana Meehan was speaking at a "Women and Men in the Media" conference at the National Press Club in Washington, D.C., on April 10, 1989. According to Daren C. Brabham, research has also found that women's "social marginality in open scientific problem solving is an advantage" because as "outsiders," they are able "to see novel solutions to problems" that "experts at the center of a scientific domain are less likely to see." *Crowdsourcing*, 21.

51. Linda Coughlin, Ellen Wingard, and Keith Hallihan, eds. "Introduction," in *Enlightened Power: How Women Are Transforming the Practice of Leadership* (Jossey-Bass, 2005), 15.

52. Bruffee, *Collaborative Learning*, 5. Helen E. Fisher notes that the feminine disposition "to work in egalitarian teams, network, and support others [was] unquestionably vital to ancestral women who needed to support one another and their children." Coughlin et al., *Enlightened Power*, 138.

53. McKnight and Block refer to an "abundant community," one in which people combine and organize their gifts. *The Abundant Community*, 74. McKnight argues that the self-help movement has been partly due to "the limits" of "professional helpers" and even the "disabling effects of their services" (p. 16). On the other hand, Robert Putnam reported that a study of California self-help groups found that 60 percent had "professional leaders." *Bowling Alone: The Collapse and Revival of American Community* (Simon & Schuster, 2000), 150–51. There is a blurring here of the distinction between self-help and support groups.

54. Barker and Brown, *A Different Kind of Politics*, 62.

55. inside.augsburg.edu/janeaddams/ (8/9/13).

56. Ibid.

57. Nan Kari and Nan Skelton, eds., *Voices of Hope: The Story of the Jane Addams School for Democracy* (Kettering Foundation Press, 2007), 133.

58. Ibid., 6.

59. Ibid., 13, 14.

60. Ibid., 24.

61. Ibid., 3.

62. Ibid., 138.

63. Philip Slater, *The Pursuit of Loneliness: American Culture at the Breaking Point* (Beacon Press, 1970), 4.

64. James Buchanan, *The Limits of Liberty* (University of Chicago Press, 1975), 78.

Selected Bibliography

Addams, Jane. *The Second Twenty Years at Hull House.* The Macmillan Company, 1930.

Addams, Jane. *Twenty Years at Hull-House.* The Macmillan Company, 1910.

Anderson, Charles W. *Prescribing the Life of the Mind: An Essay on the Purpose of the University, the Aims of Liberal Education, the Competence of Citizens, and the Cultivation of Practical Reason.* University of Wisconsin Press, 1993.

Anderson, Chris. *The Long Tail: Why the Future of Business is Selling Less of More.* Hyperion, 2006.

Arum, Richard, and Josipa Roksa. *Academically Adrift: Limited Learning on College Campuses.* University of Chicago Press. 2011.

Axelrod, Robert. *The Complexity of Cooperation: Agent-Based Models, Competition and Collaboration.* Princeton University Press, 1997.

Ball, Philip. *Critical Mass: How One Thing Leads to Another.* Farrar, Straus and Giroux, 2004.

Banner, Stuart. *American Property: A History of How, Why, and What We Own.* Harvard University Press, 2011.

Barber, Benjamin R. *Strong Democracy: Participatory Politics for a New Age.* University of California Press, 1984.

Barker, Derek W. M., and David W. Brown, eds. *A Different Kind of Politics: Readings on the Role of Higher Education in Democracy.* Kettering Foundation Press, 2009.

Barker, Derek W. M., Noelle McAfee, and David W. McIver, eds. *Democratizing Deliberation: A Political Theory Anthology.* Kettering Foundation Press, 2012.

Barrett, William. *The Illusions of Technique.* Anchor Books, 1979.

Barzun, Jacques. "The Professions Under Siege." *Harper's* (October 1978): 236, 231–236, 268.

Bellah, Robert N., Richard Madsen, William M. Sullivan, Ann Swidler, and Stephen M. Tipton. *Habits of the Heart: Individualism and Commitment in American Life.* University of California Press, 1985.

Bender, Thomas. *Intellect and Public Life: Essays on the Social History of Academic Intellectuals in the United States.* Johns Hopkins University Press, 1993.

Bender, Thomas, and Carl E. Schorske, eds. *American Academic Culture in Transformation: Fifty Years, Four Disciplines.* Princeton University Press, 1997.

Benson, Lee, Ira Harkavy, and John Puckett. "Democratic Transformation Through University-Assisted Schools. In *"To Serve a Larger Purpose:" Engagement for Democracy and the Transformation of Higher Education,* edited by John Saltmarsh and Matthew Hartley, 49–81. Temple University Press, 2011.

Bentley, Alex, Mark Earls, and Michael J. O'Brien. *I'll Have What She's Having: Mapping Social Behavior.* MIT Press, 2011.

Berger, Peter L., and Thomas Luckman. *The Social Construction of Reality.* Random House, 1966.

Bernstein R.B. *Thomas Jefferson.* Oxford University Press, 2003.

Bishop, Bill. *The Big Sort: Why the Clustering of Like-Minded America Is Tearing Us Apart.* Houghton Mifflin, 2008.

Blau, Melinda, and Karen L. Fingerman. *Consequential Strangers: The Power of People Who Don't Seem to Matter . . . But Really Do.* W. W. Norton, 2009.

Bledstein, Burton J. *The Culture of Professionalism: The Middle Class and the Development of Higher Education in America.* W. W. Norton, 1978.

Boorstin, Daniel J. *Democracy and Its Discontents: Reflections on Everyday America.* Random House, 1974.

Bowen, William G. *Higher Education in the Digital Age.* Princeton University Press, 2013.

Boyte, Harry C. "Civic Agency and the Cult of the Expert." A Study for the Kettering Foundation, 2009.

Boyte, Harry C. *Commonwealth: A Return to Citizen Politics.* Free Press, 1989.

Boyte, Harry C. *Everyday Politics.* University of Pennsylvania Press. 2004.

Boyte, Harry C. "Higher Education and the American Commonwealth Partnership: An Interview with Harry Boyte." *Higher Education Exchange* (2012): 4–12.

Boyte, Harry C. "Public Work: Civic Populism Versus Technocracy in Higher Education." In *Agent of Democracy: Higher Education and the HEX Journey,* edited by David W. Brown and Deborah Witte. Kettering Foundation Press, 2008.

Boyte, Harry C. "Reinventing Citizenship as Public Work." A Study for the Kettering Foundation, 2013.

Brabham, Daren C. *Crowdsourcing.* MIT Press, 2013.

Brann, Eva T. H. *Paradoxes of Education in a Republic.* University of Chicago Press, 1979.

Brint, Steven. *In the Age of Experts: The Changing Role of Professionals in Politics and Public Life.* Princeton University Press, 1994.

Brown, David Warfield. *The Real Change-Makers: Why Government Is Not the Problem or the Solution.* Praeger, 2012.

Brown, David W. "Daring To Be Unprofessional." *Higher Education Exchange* (1997): 10–13.

Brown, David W. "The Journey of a Recovering Professional." *Higher Education Exchange* (2008): 5–12.

Brown, David W. *Organization Smarts: Portable Skills for Professionals Who Want to Get Ahead.* AMACOM, 2002.

Brown, David W. "Professional Virtue: A Dangerous Kind of Humbug." *Change* (November/December, 1985): 8–9, 46–47.

Brown, David W. "Talking the Walk: Making Sense of HEX (1994–2004)." *Higher Education Exchange* (2004): 5–16.

Brown, David W. *When Strangers Cooperate: Using Social Conventions to Govern Ourselves.* Free Press, 1995.

Brown, John Seely, and Paul Duguid. *The Social Life of Information.* Harvard Business School Publishing, 2002.

Bruffee, Kenneth. *Collaborative Learning: Higher Education, Interdependence and the Authority of Knowledge.* Johns Hopkins University Press, 1993.

Buchan, James. *The Authentic Adam Smith: His Life and Ideas.* W. W. Norton, 2006. Buchanan, James. *The Limits of Liberty.* University of Chicago Press, 1975.

Burger, Edward B., and Michael Starbird. *Coincidences, Chaos, and All That Math Jazz.* W. W. Norton, 2005.

Butin, Dan W., and Scott Seider eds. *The Engaged Campus: Certificates, Minors, and Majors as the New Community Engagement.* Palgrave Macmillan, 2012.

Carcasson, Martin. "Facilitating Community Democracy from Campus: Centers, Faculty, and Students as Key Resources of Passionate Impartiality." *Higher Education Exchange* (2010): 15–26.

Carr, Nicholas. *The Shallows: What the Internet Is Doing to Our Brains.* W. W. Norton, 2010.

Challenger, Douglas. "The New England Center for Civic Life: A Decade of Making a Difference" In *Agent of Democracy: Higher Education and the HEX Journey,* edited by David W. Brown and Deborah Witte. Kettering Foundation Press, 2008.

Challenger, Douglas, and Joni Doherty. "Living in the Lap of an Immense Intelligence." *Higher Education Exchange* (2002): 54–71.

Clark, Burton. *The Higher Education System: Academic Organization in Cross-National Perspective.* University of California Press, 1983.

Cohen, Jeremy, ed. "A Laboratory for Public Scholarship and Democracy: New Directions for Teaching and Learning," Jossey-Bass (April 2006).

Cohen, Joshua T., Peter J. Neumann, and Milton C. Weinstein. "Does Preventive Care Save Money? Health Economics and the Presidential Candidates." *The New England Journal of Medicine* (February 14, 2008): 661–63.

Collins, Randall. *The Credential Society: An Historical Sociology of Education and Stratification*. Academic Press, 1979.

Corson, John J. *The Governance of Colleges and Universities*. McGraw-Hill, 1975.

Coughlin, Linda, Ellen Wingard, and Keith Hallihan, eds. *Enlightened Power: How Women Are Transforming the Practice of Leadership*. Jossey-Bass, 2005.

Cremin, Lawrence A. *American Education: The Colonial Experience*. Harper & Row, 1970.

Cremin, Lawrence A. *American Education: The Metropolitan Experience, 1876–1980*. Harper & Row, 1988.

Cremin, Lawrence A. *Popular Education and Its Discontents*. Harper & Row, 1989.

Cremin, Lawrence A. *Traditions of American Education*. Basic Books, 1977.

Crenson, Matthew A., and Benjamin Ginsberg. *Downsizing Democracy: How America Sidelined Its Citizens and Privatized Its Public*. Johns Hopkins University Press, 2004.

Crick, Bernard. *In Defence of Politics*. 2nd ed. University of Chicago Press, 1972.

Daedalus. "On Professions and Professionals." *Journal of the American Academy of Arts and Sciences* (Summer, 2005): 13–75.

Damrosch, David. *We Scholars: Changing the Culture of the University*. Harvard University Press, 1995.

Delbanco, Andrew. *College: What It Was, Is, and Should Be*. Harvard University Press, 2012.

Dewey, John. *Experience and Education*. Collier Books, 1938.

Dewey, John. *The Quest for Certainty*. Paragon Books, G. P. Putnam's Sons, 1979.

Dionne, E. J. Jr. *Our Divided Political Heart: The Battle for the American Idea in an Age of Discontent*. Bloomsbury, 2012.

Dzur, Albert W. *Democratic Professionalism: Citizen Participation and the Reconstruction of Professional Ethics, Identity and Practice*. Pennsylvania State University Press, 2008.

Dzur, Albert W. *Punishment, Participatory Democracy and the Jury*. Oxford University Press, 2012.

Ellickson, Robert C. *Order Without Law: How Neighbors Settle Disputes*. Harvard University Press, 1991.

Elshtain, Jean Bethke. *Jane Addams and the Dream of American Democracy: A Life*. Basic Books, 2002.

Elster, Jon. *Nuts and Bolts for the Social Sciences*. Cambridge University Press, 1989.

Emerson, Ralph Waldo. "The American Scholar." In *Selections from Ralph Waldo Emerson*, edited by Stephen E. Whicher. Houghton Mifflin, 1960.

Emerson, Ralph Waldo. "The American Scholar," in *The American Tradition of Literature*. W. W. Norton, 1961: 147–168.

Evans, Sara M., and Harry C. Boyte. *Free Spaces: The Sources of Democratic Change in America*. Harper & Row, 1986.

Ferguson, Andrew Guthrie. *Why Jury Duty Matters: A Citizen's Guide to Constitutional Action*. New York University Press, 2013.

Fine, Allison. *Momentum: Igniting Social Change in the Connected Age*. Jossey-Bass, 2006.

Firestein, Stuart. *Ignorance: How It Drives Science*. Oxford University Press, 2012.

Fischer, Claude S. *Made in America: A Social History of American Culture and Character*. University of Chicago Press, 2010.

Flacks, Richard. *Making History: The American Left and the American Mind*. Columbia University Press, 1988.

Flyvbjerg, Bent. *Making Social Science Matter: Why Social Inquiry Fails and How It Can Succeed Again*. Cambridge University Press, 2001.

Forrester, John. *The Deliberative Practitioner: Encouraging Participatory Planning Processes*. MIT Press, 2000.

Gardner, Susan K., and Pilar Mendoza, eds. *On Becoming a Scholar: Socialization and Development in Doctoral Education*. Stylus, 2010.

Gastil, John, E., Pierre Deess, Philip J. Weiser, and Cindy Simmons. *The Jury and Democracy: How Jury Deliberation Promotes Civic Engagement and Political Participation*. Oxford University Press, 2010.

Geertz, Clifford. *Local Knowledge: Further Essays in Interpretive Anthropology*. Basic Books, 1983.

Gibbons, Michael, Camille Limoges, Helga Nowotny, Simon Schwartzman, Peter Scott, and Martin Trow. *The New Production of Knowledge: The Dynamics of Science and Research in Contemporary Societies*. Sage Publications, 1994.

Gilligan, Carol. *In a Different Voice: Psychological Theory and Women's Development*. Harvard University Press, 1982.

Gladwell, Malcolm. *The Tipping Point: How Little Things Can Make a Big Difference*. Little, Brown, 2000.

Gladwell, Malcolm. *Outliers: The Story of Success*. Little, Brown, 2008.

Golde, Chris. "Entering Different Worlds: Socialization into Disciplinary Communities." In *On Becoming A Scholar: Socialization and Development in Doctoral Education*, edited by Susan K. Gardner and Pilar Mendoza, 79–95. Stylus, 2010.

Graff, Gerald. *Beyond the Culture Wars: How Teaching the Conflicts Can Revitalize American Education*. W. W. Norton, 1992.

Graff, Gerald. *Clueless in Academe: How Schooling Obscures the Life of the Mind.* Yale University Press, 2003.

Gutmann, Amy, and Dennis Thompson. *Democracy and Disagreement.* Harvard University Press, 1997.

Haber, Samuel. *The Quest for Authority and Honor in the American Professions, 1750–1900.* University of Chicago Press, 1991.

Habermas, Jurgen. *Theory and Practice.* Beacon Press, 1974.

Hamilton, Edith. *The Greek Way to Civilization.* Mentor Books, 1960.

Hanson, William. *Smart Medicine: How the Changing Role of Doctors Will Revolutionize Health Care.* Palgrave Macmillan, 2011.

Harper, Steven J. *The Lawyer Bubble: A Profession in Crisis.* Basic Books, 2013.

Haskell, Thomas L. *The Emergence of Professional Social Science: The American Social Science Association and the Nineteenth-Century Crisis of Authority.* Johns Hopkins University Press, 1977.

Haskell, Thomas L. *Objectivity Is Not Neutrality: Explanatory Schemes in History.* Johns Hopkins University Press, 2000.

Hayek, Frederick. *The Constitution of Liberty.* University of Chicago Press, Phoenix Edition, 1978.

Hayes, Christopher. *The Twilight of the Elites: America After Meritocracy.* Crown Publishers, 2012.

Helgesen, Sally. *The Female Advantage: Women's Ways of Leadership.* Currency Doubleday, 1995.

Hindman, Matthew. *The Myth of Digital Democracy.* Princeton University Press, 2010.

Hirsch, Fred. *Social Limits to Growth.* Academic Press, 1976.

Hirschman, Albert O. *Shifting Involvements: Private Interest and Public Action.* Princeton University Press, 1982.

Hitt, Jack. *Bunch of Amateurs.* Crown Publishers, 2012.

Hofstadter, Richard. *Anti-Intellectualism in American Life.* Vintage Books, 1963.

Holland, John H. *Emergence: From Chaos to Order.* Addison-Wesley, 1998.

Illich, Ivan. *Disabling Professions.* Marion Boyars, 1978.

Jencks, Christopher, and David Riesman. *The Academic Revolution.* University of Chicago Press, 1977.

Johnson, Steven. *Emergence: The Connected Lives of Ants, Brains, Cities and Software.* Scribner, 2001.

Jonakait, Randolph N. *The American Jury System.* Yale University Press, 2003.

Kari, Nan, and Nan Skelton ed. *The Story of Jane Addams School for Democracy.* Kettering Foundation Press, 2007.

Keen, Andrew. *The Cult of the Amateur: How Today's Internet is Killing Our Culture.* Doubleday/Currency, 2007.

Kingston, Robert, and Peter Levine. "What is 'Public' About What Academics Do? An Exchange with Robert Kingston and Peter Levine." *Higher Education Exchange* (2004): 17–29.

Knight Louise, W. *Citizen: Jane Addams and the Struggle for Democracy.* University of Chicago Press, 2005.

Knutsen, Ellen M., and Dan A. Lewis. "Civic Engagement and Doctoral Education." *Higher Education Exchange* (2012): 48–53.

Kuhn, Thomas S. *The Structure of Scientific Revolutions.* Second Edition. University of Chicago Press, 1970.

Kytle, Jackson. *To Want to Learn: Insights and Provocations for Engaged Learning.* Palgrave Macmillan, 2004.

Labaree, David F. *How to Succeed in School Without Really Trying.* Yale University Press, 1997.

Leighninger, Matt. *The Next Form of Democracy: How Expert Rule Is Giving Way to Shared Governance . . . and Why Politics Will Never Be the Same.* Vanderbilt University Press, 2006.

Leighninger, Matt. "Citizen-Centered Democracy: An Interview with Matt Leighninger." *Higher Education Exchange* (2009): 14–22.

Leighninger, Matt. "Mapping Deliberative Civic Engagement: Pictures from a (R)evolution." In *Democracy in Motion: Evaluating the Practice and Impact of Deliberative Civic Engagement,* edited by Tina Nabatchi, John Gastil, G. Michael Weiksner, and Matt Leighninger, 19–39. Oxford University Press, 2012.

Lewis, David. *Convention: A Philosophical Study.* Harvard University Press, 1969.

Macey, Jonathan, R. *The Death of Corporate Reputation; How Integrity Has Been Destroyed on Wall Street.* Financial Times Press, 2013.

Mansbridge, Jane J., ed. *Beyond Self-Interest.* University of Chicago Press, 1990.

Marmor, Andrei. *Social Conventions: From Language to Law.* Princeton University Press, 2009.

Maslow, Abraham. *The Psychology of Science.* Harper & Row, 1966.

Mathews, David. *The Ecology of Democracy: Finding Ways to Have a Stronger Hand in Shaping Our Future.* Kettering Foundation Press, 2014.

Mathews, David. *Politics for People: Finding a Responsible Public Voice.* University of Illinois Press, 1994.

McAfee, Noelle. "Public Scholarship, or How to Assist in the Autopoiesis of Political Communities." *Higher Education Exchange* (2009): 5–13.

McDaniels, Melissa. "Doctoral Socialization for Teaching Roles.," In *On Becoming a Scholar: Socialization and Development in Doctoral Education,* edited by Susan K. Gardner and Pilar Mendozo, 29–44. Stylus, 2010.

McKnight, John. *The Careless Society: Community and Its Counterfeits.* Basic Books. 1995.

McKnight, John. "Professionalized Service and Disabling Help." In Ivan Illich, *Disabling Professions*, 69–91. Marion Boyars, 1978.

McKnight, John. "Regenerating Community." *Social Policy* (Winter 1987): 54–58.

McKnight, John, and Peter Block. *The Abundant Community: Awakening the Power of Families and Neighborhoods.* Berrett-Koehler, 2010.

Menand, Louis. *The Metaphysical Club: A Story of Ideas in America.* Farrar, Straus and Giroux, 2001.

Mendoza Pilar, and Susan K. Gardner. "The Ph.D in the United States." In *On Becoming a Scholar: Socialization and Development in Doctoral Education,* edited by Susan K. Gardner and Pilar Mendoza, 11–26. Stylus, 2010.

Merton, Robert K. *Social Theory and Social Structures.* Free Press, 1968.

Miller, Matt. *The Tyranny of Dead Ideas: Revolutionary Thinking for a New Age of Prosperity.* Henry Holt, 2010.

Mitchell, Melanie. *Complexity: A Guided Tour.* Oxford University Press, 2009.

Morone, James A. *The Democratic Wish: Popular Participation and the Limits of American Government.* Yale University Press, 1998.

Nabatchi, Tina, John Gastil, G. Michael Weiksner, and Matt Leighninger, eds. *Democracy in Motion: Evaluating the Practice and Impact of Deliberative Civic Engagement.* Oxford University Press, 2012.

Oakeshott, Michael. *The Voice of Liberal Learning: Michael Oakeshott on Education,* edited by Timothy Fuller. Yale University Press, 1989.

O'Meara, KerryAnn. "Engaged Faculty: An Interview with KerryAnn O'Meara." *Higher Education Exchange* (2011): 14–23.

Ostrom, Elinor. *Governing the Commons: The Evolution of Institutions for Collective Action.* Cambridge University Press, 1990.

Page, Scott. *The Difference: How the Power of Diversity Creates Better Groups, Firms, Schools, and Societies.* Princeton University Press, 2007.

Palmer, Parker J. *The Courage to Teach: Exploring the Inner Landscape of a Teacher's Life.* Jossey-Bass, 1998.

Palmer, Parker J. *Healing the Heart of Democracy: The Courage to Create a Politics Worthy of the Human Spirit.* Jossey-Bass, 2011.

Parsons, Talcott. "The Academic System: A Sociologist's View" *Public Interest.* 13 (Fall 1968): 173–97.

Percy, Walker. *The Message in the Bottle.* Farrar, Straus and Giroux, 1977.

Perry, Lewis. *Intellectual Life in America: A History.* University of Chicago Press, 1989.

Polanyi, Michael. *Personal Knowledge: Towards a Post-Critical Philosophy.* University of Chicago Press, 1962.

Polanyi, Michael. "Tacit Knowing: Its Bearing on Some Problems of Philosophy." *Review of Modern Physics* 34 (October 1962): 601–16.

Polanyi, Michael, and Harry Prosch. *Meaning*. University of Chicago Press, 1975.

Polletta, Francesca. *It Was Like a Fever*. University of Chicago Press, 2006.

Price, Don K. *The Scientific Estate*. Belknap Press, 1965.

Purdy, Jedediah. *The Meaning of Property: Freedom, Community, and the Legal Imagination*. Yale University Press, 2010.

Putnam, Robert D. *Bowling Alone: The Collapse and Revival of American Community*. Simon and Schuster, 2000.

Raymond, Eric S. *The Cathedral and the Bazaar: Musings on Linux and Open Source by an Accidental Revolutionary*. O'Reilly, 2001.

Rheingold, Howard. *Smart Mobs: The Next Social Revolution*. Basic Books, 2002.

Riesman, David. "Some Observations on Community Plans and Utopia." *Yale Law Journal* 57, no. 2 (Dececmeber 1947): 173–200.

Rosovsky, Henry. *The University: An Owner's Manual*. W. W. Norton, 1990.

Saltmarsh, John, and Mathew Hartley, eds. In *"To Serve a Larger Purpose": Engagement for Democracy and the Transformation of Higher Education*. Temple University Press, 2011.

Sandel, Michael J. *Democracy's Discontent: America in Search of a Public Philosophy*. Belknap Press of the Harvard University Press, 1996.

Sandel, Michael J. *What Money Can't Buy: The Moral Limits of Markets*. Farrar, Straus and Giroux, 2012.

Sanders, Lynn M. "Against Deliberation." *Political Theory* 25 (1997): 347–76.

Schein, Edgar, H. *The Corporate Culture Survival Guide: Sense and Nonsense About Culture Change*. Jossey-Bass, 1999.

Schelling, Thomas C. *Micromotives and Macrobehavior*. W. W. Norton, 1978.

Schon, Donald A. *Educating the Reflective Practitioner*. Jossey-Bass, 1987.

Schon, Donald A. *The Reflective Practitioner: How Professionals Think in Action*. Basic Books, 1983.

Schrage, Michael. *Serious Play: How the World's Best Companies Simulate to Innovate*. Harvard Business School Press, 2000.

Schwartz, Barry. *The Battle for Human Nature: Science, Morality and Modern Life*. W. W. Norton, 1986.

Scott, James C. *Seeing Like A State: How Certain Schemes to Improve the Human Condition Have Failed*. Yale University Press, 1998.

Sennett, Richard. *Together: The Rituals, Pleasures and Politics of Cooperation*. Yale University Press, 2012.

Shaffer, Marguerite. "Changing Public Culture: An Interview with Marguerite S. Shaffer." *Higher Education Exchange* (2008): 23–38.

Sherden, William A. *The Fortune Sellers: The Big Business of Buying and Selling Predictions*. John Wiley & Sons, 1998.

Shinew, Dawn, and Tami Moore. "Exploring Epistemological Diversity in a Doctoral Seminar." In *On Becoming a Scholar: Socialization and Development in*

Doctoral Education, edited by Susan K. Gardner and Pilar Mendoza, 243–63. Stylus, 2010.

Shirky, Clay. *Cognitive Surplus: Creativity and Generosity in a Connected Age.* Penguin Press, 2010.

Shirky, Clay. *Here Comes Everybody: The Power of Organizing Without Organizations.* Penguin Press, 2008.

Silver, Nate. *The Signal and the Noise: Why So Many Predictions Fail—But Some Don't.* Penguin Press, 2012.

Slater, Philip. *The Pursuit of Loneliness: American Culture at the Breaking Point.* Beacon Press, 1970.

Smith, Adam. *The Wealth of Nations.* Penguin Books, 1977.

Smith, J. Walker, and Ann Clurman, *Generation Ageless: How Baby Boomers Are Changing the Way We Live Today . . . and They're Just Getting Started.* HarperCollins, 2007.

Sowell, Thomas. *Knowledge and Decisions.* Basic Books, 1980.

Sugden, Robert. "Spontaneous Order." *Journal of Economic Perspective* 3, no. 4 (Fall 1989): 85–97.

Sullivan, William S. *Work and Integrity: The Crisis and Promise of Professionalism in America.* Harper Collins, 1995.

Surowiecki, James. *The Wisdom of Crowds: Why the Many Are Smarter Than the Few and How Collective Wisdom Shapes Business, Economies, Societies and Nations.* Doubleday, 2004.

Tamanaha, Brian Z. *Failing Law Schools.* University of Chicago Press, 2012.

Tetlock, Philip. *Expert Political Judgment: How Good Is It? How Can We Know?* Princeton University Press, 2005.

Thomas, Nancy, and Peter Levine, "Deliberative Democracy and Higher Education: Higher Education's Democratic Mission." In *To Serve a Larger Purpose: Engagement for Democracy and the Transformation of Higher Education,* edited by John Saltmarsh and Mathew Hartley, 154–76. Temple University Press, 2011.

Tocqueville, Alexis de. *Democracy in America,* translated by George Lawrence, edited by J. P. Mayer. Doubleday Anchor Books, 1969.

Trilling, Lionel. *Beyond Culture: Essays on Literature and Learning.* Harcourt Brace, 1979.

Ullmann-Margalit, Edna. *The Emergence of Norms.* Oxford University Press, 1977.

Waldrop, M. Mitchell. *Complexity: The Emerging Science at the Edge of Order and Chaos.* Simon & Schuster, 1992.

Walzer, Michael. *Spheres of Justice: A Defense of Pluralism and Equality.* Basic Books, 1983.

Ward, Kelly. "Doctoral Student Socialization for Service." In *On Becoming a Scholar: Socialization and Development in Doctoral Education*, edited by Susan K. Gardner and Pilar Mendoza. Stylus, 57–76. 2010.

Watts, Duncan. *Six Degrees: The Science of a Connected Age*. W. W. Norton, 2013.

Weber, Steven. *The Success of Open Source*. Harvard University Press, 2004.

Weinberg, Adam. "Public Work at Colgate: An Interview with Adam Weinberg." In *Agent of Democracy: Higher Education and the HEX Journey*, edited by David W. Brown and Deborah Witte, 103–18. Kettering Foundation Press, 2008.

Weinberger, David. *Everything Is Miscellaneous: The Power of the New Digital Disorder*. Times Books, Henry Holt and Company, 2007.

Weinberger, David. *Too Big To Know: Rethinking Knowledge Now That the Facts Aren't the Facts, Experts Are Everywhere, and the Smartest Person in the Room Is the Room*. Basic Books, 2011.

Westbrook, Robert B. *John Dewey and American Democracy*. Cornell University Press, 1991.

Whitehead, Alfred North. *The Aims of Education*. Free Press, 1967.

Whitehead, Alfred North. *Science and the Modern World*. Free Press, 1967.

Wiebe, Robert H. *Self-Rule: A Cultural History of American Democracy*. University of Chicago Press, 1995.

Wilensky, Harold. "The Professionalization of Everyone?" *The American Journal of Sociology*, LXX, no. 2 (September 1964): 137–58.

Wilentz, Sean. *The Rise of American Democracy: Jefferson to Lincoln*. W. W. Norton, 2005.

Wilshire, Bruce. *The Moral Collapse of the University: Professionalism, Purity, and Alienation*. State University of New York Press, 1990.

Wilson, Mark, and Nan Fairley, "Living Democracy: A Project for Students and Citizens." *Higher Education Exchange* (2012): 35–47.

Wright, Wynne. "Wicked Bedfellows: Can Science and Democracy Coexist in the Land Grant?" *Higher Education Exchange* (2012): 59–68.

Zey, Mary. *Rational Choice Theory and Organizational Theory: A Critique*. Sage Publications, 1997.

Index